PRAISE FOR *HOTEL* BY JOANNA WALSH:

Evocative ... Walsh's strange, probing book is all the more affecting for eschewing easy resolution.

Walsh's writing has intellectual rigour and bags of formal bravery ... *Hotel* is a boldly intellectual work that repays careful reading. Its semiotic wordplay, circling prose and experimental form may prove a refined taste, but in its deft delineation of a complex modern phenomenon—and, perhaps, a modern malaise—it's a great success.

Walsh has been praised to the skies by Chris Kraus and Jeff Vandermeer, and it isn't hard to see why. Her writing sways between the tense and the absurd, as if it's hovering between this world and another.

PRAISE FOR *DRONE* BY ADAM ROTHSTEIN:

Adam Rothstein's primer on drones covers (such themes as) the representation of drones in science fiction and popular culture. The technological aspects are covered in detail, and there is interesting discussion of the way in which our understanding of technology is grounded in historical narratives. As Rothstein writes, the attempt to draw a boundary between one technology and another often ignores the fact that new technologies are not quite as new as we think.

OBJECTLESSONS

A book series about the hidden lives of ordinary things.

Series Editors:

Ian Bogost and Christopher Schaberg

Advisory Board:

Sara Ahmed, Jane Bennett, Jeffrey Jerome Cohen,
Johanna Drucker, Raiford Guins, Graham Harman,
renée hoogland, Pam Houston, Eileen Joy, Douglas
Kahn, Daniel Miller, Esther Milne, Timothy Morton,
Kathleen Stewart, Nigel Thrift, Rob Walker, Michele White.

In association with

LOYOLA
UNIVERSITY
NEW ORLEANS

Georgia
Tech

Center for
Media Studies

BOOKS IN THE SERIES

dust

MICHAEL MARDER

Bloomsbury Academic
An imprint of Bloomsbury Publishing Inc

B L O O M S B U R Y
NEW YORK · LONDON · OXFORD · NEW DELHI · SYDNEY

Bloomsbury Academic
An imprint of Bloomsbury Publishing Inc

1385 Broadway
New York
NY 10018
USA

50 Bedford Square
London
WC1B 3DP
UK

www.bloomsbury.com

**BLOOMSBURY and the Diana logo are trademarks of
Bloomsbury Publishing Plc**

First published 2016

Library of Congress Cataloging-in-Publication Data
Marder, Michael, 1980-
Dust/Michael Marder.
pages cm. – (Object lessons)
Includes bibliographical references and index.
ISBN 978-1-62892-558-6 (pbk.: alk. paper) – ISBN 978-1-62892-171-7
(hardback: alk. paper) 1. Dust. 2. Cosmic dust. 3. Allergens. 4. Sweeping and
dusting. 5. Particles I. Title.
TD884.5.M37 2016
551.51'13–dc23
2015024508

ISBN: PB: 978-1-6289-2558-6
ePub: 978-1-6289-2594-4
ePDF: 978-1-6289-2330-8

Series: Object Lessons

Typeset by Deanta Global Publishing Services, Chennai, India
Printed and bound in the United States of America

For Marina and Lisete

CONTENTS

TO THE READER

No matter how desperately you fight against it,
dust pervades everything.
It accumulates in fuzzy balls or gathers in even layers,
adapting to the contours of things
and marking the passage of time.
In itself, it is also a gathering place,
a random community of what has been and what is yet to be,
a catalog of traces, an inventory of threats,
and a set of promises:
cosmic residue and industrial réfuse, dead skin cells and
plant pollen,
hair and paper fibers, not to mention the bacteria and
dust mites
who make it their home.
Dust crosses the boundaries between the living and the dead,
plant and animal matter, the earth and the sky,
the inside and the outside, you and the world
("for dust thou art, and unto dust shalt thou return").
What does it smuggle
in each of these crossings?

As you step over the threshold of this book,
a piece of advice on what to do
when you are through with it.
After flipping the last page,
put it down and let it gather dust
on a shelf
or on a coffee table.
Lots of dust.
So that it, too, would mutely commune
with the very things it describes.

M. M.

1 DUSTING

"Don't forget me," whispers the settled dust to the hand with the cloth, and the wet cloth absorbs this whisper.
—JOSEPH BRODSKY, "NORTH OF DELPHI"

a gem of a word

Words are little gems scattered in the gutters of everyday life. Too lazy or too hurried, we regularly pass them unnoticed; utter and jot them down absentmindedly; speak *through* them, but not *of* them, unless we compose poetry or (certain strands of) philosophy. *Dusting* is one of these gems. Let us, then, pick it up, dust it, rotate it in our hands and in our minds, taking the time to appreciate how its many dimensions refract and absorb the light of meaning. What the word itself tells us and what it withholds from us will be vital to everything that follows.

Much depends on whether we hear in *dusting* a noun or a verb in the form of a gerund. If dusting is a thing, then it refers to a thin layer or to a sparse application of any sort of loose stuff, such as powder or snow. If, conversely, it is an activity, then it means wiping dust away from furniture and from all the other things that line our homes. Even as a verb, it encompasses several apparently discordant senses. On the one hand, we have "to wipe dust away from something" (e.g., to dust a cupboard), and, on the other hand, "to sprinkle with powder or dust" (e.g., to dust grass with insecticide), "to apply dust." To dust something is, at once, to add and to remove that which lends this occupation its name.[1] Dusting is also undusting, to revive a nearly obsolete Shakespearian word.

Provided that the context of its use is unknown or stays indeterminate, *dusting* denotes two opposite things, in the same stroke saying and unsaying, contra-dicting, itself. It introduces a glitch into the well-oiled mechanisms of economic and symbolic exchanges through an exorbitant procedure, according to which to clear dust away entails, in effect, to strew this same substance around. Upsetting our prior expectations, the word gives us to understand that it will guard its secret, will not reveal itself to us with any degree of satisfaction, will scarcely become transparent. It covers itself with coats of dust, oblivious to our timid preparations for dusting it.

Georg Wilhelm Friedrich Hegel admired words with mutually exclusive significations. The reason behind his enthusiasm was that, in them, he espied concrete linguistic supports for his speculative dialectical philosophy, dependent upon the self-negation of concepts. I am certain that he would have loved *dusting*, because its substantive sense subverts its verbal counterpart and because the verb both affirms and denies itself. But what exactly can we infer from this tension that animates thought, permeates language, and makes its semantic strings vibrate?

The word we are poring over whispers to us that the more we dust things in an effort to clean them, the more dust will be unsettled, spreading through the air, gravitating toward other things and finding a provisional abode on their tops, only to drift away again at the next opportunity. Dusting does not eliminate but redistributes dust. Less thick right here, it is more concentrated over there, for the time being. We cannot liquidate dust for good since—our desire to "clean" it notwithstanding—we simply perturb and move this unbearably light garbage from one place to another. Opposing something internally opposed to itself, we wage a losing battle, in which dust gives us a thorough dusting. Whatever the menaces and the promises it harbors, we can rest assured that it will eternally return, not as suddenly and dramatically as a haunting ghost but quietly and cumulatively, like the falling snow.

Dusting is thus a self-defeating occupation, especially if judged based on the success with which it attains its goals. It spearheads a doomed fight against dispersed dry matter whose particles will choose another spot to land upon after a duster has disturbed their brief repose. When it comes to dusters, the use of these mediating devices does nothing to put an end to dust's maddening dance; a sponge, a mop, and a cloth help it migrate to another surface either by attaching it to themselves or by sending it off to a different elemental milieu, notably the air. Dusters propagate dust, in lieu of eradicating it; they make it travel far and wide, for it boasts no radicle—no root—to be eradicated to begin with. Dust specks are the quintessential nomads wandering through the immensity of space, time, and sense.

Digging deeper into the origins of *dust*, we discover that it flouts the distinction between dry particles suspended in the air and pulverized moistness. Its proto-Indo-European root is *dheu*, redolent of smoke and vapor, which is also related to the German *Dunst* (mist), a cognate of the Old High German *tunst*, "storm" or "breath." A dusting braids together the elements of water, air, and earth (not to neglect the culinary uses of powdered sugar or spices). It is dry earth that, having rebelled against the heaviness of the element, is light enough to hover above and around us; a fine mist that saturates the atmosphere; a breath of matter on the brink of spirit. How to deal with it, if it is so elemental and pervasive? If it disrespects the partitions between the regions of earth and air, air and water, water and earth, nature and culture? If it is adjusted to virtually any milieu, clings and accommodates itself to the things that repel it?

The act, or the art, of dusting crisscrosses the vast fields of the elements as soon as we venture to tame dry dust with the help of a cloth and inevitably clog the air with specks that used to rest on flat surfaces, for example, of the floor or a table. When it does not hang in the air, dust mixed with moisture turns into dirt. To wit, its transmutation is anticipated in the etymology of the word, which bespeaks, via *Dunst*, something liquid. The elemental cycle of dust mimics that of water, and the work of dusting must follow suit. The *–ing* ending accentuates this unfinished process, suffused with finitude yet incomplete even after we ourselves "bite the dust." Practically and theoretically, we have no other choice but to approach dust from many angles, so as to reinitiate our contact with its interminable finitude—and, through it, with ourselves—each time anew.

face-to-face with ourselves

We contribute to the multiplication of dust with our polluting industries; by wearing clothes, using things around us, and merely living—shedding skin cells, hair, and other biological components of our bodies; and in the course of dusting the contents of our dwelling places. But we also *are* it, as the Bible and William Shakespeare tell us. The Biblical text declares in the aftermath of Adam and Eve's Fall in Genesis 3:19 that "dust thou art, and unto dust shalt thou return." Hamlet's nihilistic soliloquy in *Act Two*, Scene Two of the eponymous play asks rhetorically about the human, "What is this quintessence of dust?" Complicating the affinity between the dust outside us and the dust that we are is the fact that we usually lack the courage to examine ourselves with Biblical or Shakespearean frankness. We fail to understand that, as we clash with external dust, we displace existential anxieties and obliquely confront our mortal, rootless, restless selves, no longer discernable as such.

Let me give you an example of this strange displacement. Since household dust is comprised, mainly, of the material traces of our own bodily existence, the endeavor to eliminate it strives, quite unconsciously, to expunge vestiges of ourselves. Cloth in hand, we erase proofs of our mortality and of our posthumous blending with the environment. With the penchant for putting the house in order, desiring to bring it back to a pristine condition, dusting makes the places where we sojourn a little sterile, a tad dead, all in the name of life. In a way, this activity symbolizes our inability or our unwillingness to deal constructively with our lives, to accept their entanglements with finitude, death, and the others, archived in the dust.

My encounter with dust is a face-to-face, or surface-to-surface, meeting with myself, with parts of me that, though dead, lead an uncanny afterlife in combination with other fragmentary and whole entities, be they threads of fabric or dust mites. The very possibility of our mingling harkens back to the sharing of finite existence, against which the act of dusting rebels. (Could the Freudian "oceanic feeling," whereby, softening its boundaries, the ego melts into the world, be ever triggered by dust?) There is no depth in the encounter, save for the reciprocal mirroring effect of two surfaces: the dusting duster and the dusted dust. In most cases, nonetheless, the mirror is broken, and the former does not recognize her- or himself in the latter. A tremendous psychic investment is necessary to inhibit the flashes of traumatic self-recognition and, perversely, to identify vitality with shining, dust-free, lifeless exteriors.

If the dust outside me does not send me back to myself, to the dust that I am, then the drudgery of wiping away the footprints of past life will be strictly external, as well. I will not be guided by the question of how to dust within myself, to bring my mind to a spotless state of wonder about the world, while avoiding the sterilization of either the mind or the world. Along these lines, Henry David Thoreau narrates in *Walden*: "I had three pieces of limestone on my desk, but I was terrified to find that they required to be dusted daily, when the furniture of my mind was undusted still . . . How, then, could I have a furnished house? I would rather sit in the open air, for no dust gathers on the grass, unless where man has broken ground."[2]

A psychoanalyst would hypothesize that we avoid precisely these sorts of hard questions that invite self-analysis, or conscious work on ourselves, when we earnestly dust the physical houses, absent any reference to our psychic dwellings. In the last instance, the tremendous difficulty of "dusting the furniture of our minds" is incomparable to that of passing a cloth over an actual filing cabinet. Which is why physical dusting often substitutes for the psychic variety. Inner dusting calls for a constant interrogation of the suppositions we either hold dear or fail to notice because of their obviousness; it draws its inspiration from the ancient

Greek injunction "Know thyself!" Without revisiting, exposing, and oft-times brushing away these assumptions, as omnipresent as dust, the knowledge of everything else in the world (including the concept *world* itself) would be worthless. Or, at least, that is what an enlightened critic would tell us.

In our minds as well as in our houses, dusty realities are scorned because they represent disorder and lack of care— being unkempt. *Dusty* can also mean "old-fashioned," or "outdated." But what if the dust of thought were the disarray and the anarchy that Friedrich Nietzsche's Zarathustra recommended we cultivate in ourselves, when he said, "One must still have chaos in oneself to be able to give a birth to a dancing star"[3]? Before any constructions, let alone furniture, clog that space. Before time itself dawns in the difference between yesterday, today, and tomorrow. Nothing is outdated where there is no date to speak of. Dust is the newold or the oldnew, a zone of death *and* birth, including that of a (dancing) star.

To take the correlation between the dust that we are and the dust outside us at face value is to jump into a thicket of metaphysical issues. One of these is how we handle the materiality of existence. Thinking that our physical dwellings can be free of dust, if only for a short stretch of time, we hold onto an unarticulated belief that we, too, can become pure spirits and purge ourselves of all material trappings, first and foremost among them—the embodied mind. Ancient Greek philosopher Plotinus and the Gnostics would have subscribed to this position, which predominates in our contemporary techno-metaphysics, replete with fantasies of becoming-virtual, consigning individual consciousness to cyberspace, or uploading the data of our memories onto a more durable disk than the gray mass inside our skulls.

Especially when they plunge us into the depths of an obsession, dusting and cleaning provide escape routes from our rendezvous with ourselves. Differently put, they prevent us from facing up to our desire. The insistent movement of wiping dust away from furniture with a cloth is equivalent to caressing an inanimate object, subsequent to the cleaners' failure to give an outlet to erotic energy in meeting human flesh. The Freudian insight into dusting as an unconscious, fetishistic substitute for physical contact with another person needs no explanation. The cleaning caress stands for a loving gesture directed to things, as Gunilla Norris also intuits: "Time to dust again/Time to caress my house,/to stroke all its surfaces."[4] But, by the same token, the stroking hand sterilizes the displaced objects of affection and, thereby, subtly admits to the sterilization of the repressed desire that drives it.

Instead of a face-to-face with oneself or with a human other, an obsessive-compulsive cleaner focuses on furniture and the layers of dust superimposed on it, as though they were the acceptable, if more or less opaque, screens for the projection of forbidden fantasies and impulses. Psychic repression is so deep seated that it sets out to obliterate the coating of dust, along with what is written or projected on it, to eliminate the substratum itself, where the trace is engraved. This is the subtext of Julia Alvarez's poem "Dusting," in which the mother deletes the signatures her daughter has left in the dust ("Each morning I wrote my name/on the dusty cabinet . . ./while Mother followed, squirting/linseed from a burping can/into a crumpled-up flannel") and, above all, renders herself anonymous through heedless immersion in household chores. In contrast, the daughter's writing in the dust says *yes* to her own desire, if ephemerally and under the threat of its imminent obliteration: "But I refused with every mark/to be like her, anonymous."[5] Anonymity, without a doubt, stems from the erasure of the signature, but worse yet, it results from the destitution of the place where the inscription is left, which is not at all separate from the one who signs her name. Seeing that the human, too, is dust, writing in the dust is leaving marks on ourselves, with ourselves. To erase the possibility for such "dustography" is to discard ourselves.

I must mention in passing that, envisioning dust as a surface for inscription, I think back to my maternal grandfather, who had a peculiar habit. Whenever he visited an apartment that was untidy, he left scribbles and, sometimes, long messages written in the dust. Like a blank sheet of paper or fresh snow, evenly spread dust is a great medium for doodles and free association. (Here, in these pages, I also am writing on dust— on the subject of dust and on the actual and potential dust itself, doodling.) The projection screen need not be smooth;

it can consist of dust balls, those fluffy chunks of the real that interfere with the flawless arrangement of the house. In the contingent society of the dead and living bits of matter rolled together, one may detect the force of attraction at the heart of desire. By breaking these transient composites, dusting militates (symbolically) against desire's magnetism, allure, and basic sociability.

In addition to being full of erotic insinuations, dusting is associated with the death drive, as Freud sees it. Those who are not afraid of psychoanalytic jargon will agree that the standoff with dust *disavows* death, both acknowledging and repudiating its hold on us. The father of psychoanalysis understands the compulsion to repeat a given behavior as a fundamental attribute of organic life and its echo in our everyday existence.[6] On this view, death is the irreversible break, an event that ends the chain of mundane repetitions. Dusting is a ritual, a repetitive exercise that churns up veiled allusions to our mortality; it is a living repetition that invariably bears upon death. While, in dust, it finds the omens that existence is coming to an end, dusting rejects the glimpses of life's finitude. The small pleasure this act affords us is that of a recurrent victory over death. Fleeing from themselves, obsessive cleaners surreptitiously hope against hope for an indefinite repetition and a resurrection unencumbered with filthy matter. But all they manage to achieve is a short delay: "Quick: why aren't you dusting? On every continent we sweep floors and wipe tabletops not only to shine the place, but to forestall burial."[7]

dusting as enlightenment

Dusting the contents of our houses and apartments, we come back to the things that populate them—a chest of drawers, a bookcase, a lamp, windowsills, you name it— with an attitude dissimilar to the humdrum of pragmatic use. We touch upon them, lightly and flimsily. Our non-domineering approach exempts the dusted objects from the functions they are supposed to serve and, by virtue of their untethering, permits us to get reacquainted with them, to experience them otherwise, to see them (even if vision pales in importance as compared to touch here) through another prism, in a different light.

Stooping over a word before enunciating or writing it, we see it for what it is and feel like we are facing it for the first time. A poet or a philosopher dusts words without utilizing them, explores their usability and un-usability, at most preparing them for future usage. That is what I have done with the word "dusting" at the opening of the chapter: I have started dusting it and am still busy doing so now.

Be the dusted object a word or a thing, we are reintroduced to it by attending to its previously unnoticed edges and dimensions, lending an ear to what it dictates, and respecting its integral forms (as opposed to dust, which has no form at all). Whereas chemical cleaning agents eat into the object, artisanal dusting barely touches upon it. In and of itself, dusting ushers in an ecological comportment, above and beyond the rigid economy it is ensconced in. Not only does it aspire to make a house fit for habitation but it also refuses to impose its arbitrary rule or law (*nomos*) on the things it dusts. Retracing the contours of furniture down to the last detail, it is attuned to the manifested articulation (*logos*) of things. Its non-invasive operations are conditional upon a commitment to superficiality, an aptitude for gliding on the surface of things untroubled by their depth. Insofar as it wishes to know the world, then, dusting does not proceed further than the exposed dimensions, enabling phenomena to shine forth with their own light and to give themselves to sight again. Its ecology is wholly phenomenological.

It bears noting that dusting rituals can be as thoughtless as any other routine of daily life—and herein we find their mixed blessing. On the one hand, the temporary paralysis of "deep" thought they occasion could be beneficial. Thanks to it, we might be able, finally, to see and touch what readily offers itself, rather than try to penetrate the essence. We would, then, eschew the tendency to "overthink" existence, to dig out its buried causes and disclose its intrinsic constitution. On the other hand, dusting our houses, we seek, unbeknownst to ourselves, a sense of certainty among things, their exteriors peering from underneath the dust. We try to restore the original colors and shapes to this universe in miniature by removing anything that occludes them. In a word, we aim to disclose the things themselves, as they are, in what is tantamount to a household version of realism.

The notion of truth as lucidity, expressed in "clear and distinct ideas," *clara et distincta perceptio*, has been a staple of the European Enlightenment ever since the early modern period in the history of philosophy. Dusting takes the metaphor of clarity, which uncomfortably endures in the midst of a discourse committed to nonmetaphoric veracity, back to unmitigated literalness. Yet, a dusted object presents itself not to a disembodied mind but to the senses: above all, to vision, but also to touch. Through its recovered luminosity, the shades and textures of things show themselves as they are. Dusting is a material-phenomenological trope of the enlightenment enacting a veritable "reduction" of the sediments that conceal the real, the sediments intervening between the subject of perception and the perceived object. It discloses the façades of furniture and of everything else it cares for, so as to get to the kernel of *what is*, which is not some hidden inner essence of things, but their countenance—their first *look*.

To reiterate: dusting is surface-work oriented toward the temporarily obscured exteriors it dusts. There is no depth either to its labors or to their objectives. Indeed, the "look" of things is how phenomenologists, including Edmund Husserl and Martin Heidegger, construe the Platonic *eidos*, normally translated into English as "Idea." Far from a thought we retain in the drawer of consciousness or an independent entity located in true and unchangeable reality outside our immediate surroundings, *eidos*, the way things look, is imprinted right on the exterior of things. And, far from being transcendentally protected from decay, it fades under coats of dust. Dusting reaches over toward the skin of dusted objects, brushing them in order to get rid of foreign interferences. It wishes for the things themselves to return our look with theirs, such that nothing would stand (or lie) between them and us.

Although one can mistake the first look of a dusted word or thing for its primordial and now forgotten meaning or purpose, its "firstness," as I see it, has to do more with our attitude to these entities than with their objective makeup. The exteriors' shining forth from underneath the dust is reminiscent of the way a child experiences existence and language: with excitement and a taste for discovery; with a mixture of eagerness, uncertainty, and apprehension; without preconceptions; with all the sense organs wide open. By dusting commonplace words and things, poetry and thinking (the latter is not necessarily synonymous with philosophizing) can revive a comparable attitude toward the world, which seems to present itself to us for the first time. And then previously taken-for-granted, quotidian realities and verbal expressions are all of a sudden, almost alchemically, transubstantiated into dazzling jewels.

What I like about the allegory of dusting is that it elucidates how critique, reduction, or deconstruction cannot achieve their objectives once and for all. Just as dust will continue accumulating after every attempt to get rid of it, so prejudices and preconceptions will keep accruing after analysis (no matter how radical) shakes received ideas to the core. The labor of enlightenment and critical thinking will have to recommence every now and then, to reorganize our mental dwelling and to unblock the neglected accesses to *what is*. Trivial as it may sound, dusting, mired in finitude, is an infinite task.

Even so, it bothers me that dust tends to be portrayed in the role of a villain, as a cloud of illusion that thwarts our commerce with the real. In the next chapter, I will invite readers to imagine a positive phenomenology of dust, which gives at least as much to sight as it conceals from the eye. Suffice it to say, for now, that dust maintains things in the tightest embrace, enveloping them and entering their nooks and crannies, and that, hovering in the air, it fills the space, where we see everything else. In a postmodern spoof on the Aristotelian perfection of "thought thinking itself," on the hither side of our delusions of grandeur and anthropocentric hubris, *humans are nothing but dust looking through dust at dust*.

Even as it contends with dust, the hand that wipes a chest of drawers is urged to remain faithful to the curves, angles, and edges of the wooden structure, to stay close to them, to attend to them almost lovingly. Tidying up our houses, we receive this mission from the dust we are eager to banish, or, in other words, from the proximity of unwanted matter to a useful piece of furniture. So physically entangled are the two that the wiping hand must assiduously pass material judgments, separating the valuable from the uninvited at every stroke. To fend off the destruction of that which is useful together with the dust it treats as a nuisance, its decisions must be delicate, singular, and patient. Accordingly, it caresses: contact is vital to the sensuous enlightenment of dusting. Rendering visible presupposes a liberating touch; the "distance sense" of vision depends upon the tactile traversal of space. Epistemophilic drive, the love of knowledge rooted in Eros, flourishes from the stroking motion that dusts a room or polishes lenses so as to make them transparent, which was, incidentally, Baruch Spinoza's daytime job. Philosophy at its best, in the old sense of "the love of wisdom," is a non-invasive patting gesture, a rubbing that dusts things and our conceptions of them.

Thus far, I have hardly brushed upon life, love, and death with reference to dust. It is doubtful that another, more profound method would be better suited to the task of illuminating the invisible ties that bind the great existential themes to this nondescript réfuse. Nonetheless, let us try.

2 A PHENOMENOLOGY OF DUST

Tremulous bugle, dust that hovers where the night ends,
Golden dust hovering on the edge of visibility . . .
—FERNANDO PESSOA, "TIME'S PASSAGE"

to make space appear

Without giving it a second thought, we reach a consensus: dust is an annoyance, because it upsets the ideal orders of the house and of the universe, provokes allergies and hides the things themselves from our eyes. Just pass a flannel cloth over a dusty desk, among other pieces of furniture that surround you, to recover in one fell swoop the neatness, hygiene, and luster of your house! Released from underneath an opaque film of particles, the shine of the desk's veneer exemplifies the phenomenological conception of phenomena. Phenomena are the self-manifestations of things, as opposed to a layer of dust that underwrites obscurity and non-manifestation, gradually extinguishing the light that the things themselves irradiate. Even etymology conspires against a more positive appraisal of dust. Its Sanskrit roots, *dhvaṅs* and *dhvan*, portend "vanishing," "covering up," "enveloping or covering over," "blackening," "becoming extinguished."[1] We are, consequently, forced to conclude that dust only devours the shimmering of the objects it covers, eclipses their glow, blunts their edges, and causes their lineaments to vanish by encasing them.

But that is only half the story. We've heard enough about what dust conceals; now is the time to ask what it exposes and how.

Think about the place of dust in the translucent media of perception—the air, or light. For Plato, the third element of sight interposed between the seeing and the seen was, itself, invisible, such that its inconspicuousness could open the field of vision. Now, if this invisible "third" is populated with dust, then it is no longer completely imperceptible. Dust flakes hovering in a ray of light (say, under a lit lamp) reveal that ray, its extent and direction, along with our lived space, never as transparent as we believe. When someone passes by and perturbs their gracious swirling, illuminated with this beam, then the airflows, on which dust rides, suddenly become salient. For the atmosphere is never as static or uneventful as we suppose it to be.

Dust shows that space, traversed by barely noticeable vibrations and morsels of things, is not empty and warns us against equating it to a vacuum. It substantiates the philosophical position of Gottfried Wilhelm Leibniz, who ridiculed the thesis that a void existed in nature and who held that even microscopic units of water and air contained intricate worlds lodged within worlds within worlds. But, instead of focusing our gazes on itself, on the uncanny microcosms it houses, dust foregrounds the space it occupies. In the state of maximum exposure, it retreats from our grasp. In spite of being noticed and seen, it functions as a sign that points toward a reality outside it.

Floating in the air, dust draws our attention to space, to the in-between we habitually overlook because we single-mindedly worry about the objects that frame and crowd it. Resting on a solid surface, it emphasizes hardness, with its capacity (which is integral to the earth) for support that temporarily arrests the peregrinations of dust. Encouraging vapor condensation in the clouds, dust turns into raindrops and accentuates the proclivity to metamorphosis inherent in liquid. The evidence speaks for itself: dust is the prototype of the elements that, upon interacting with each of them, imitates them, acquires their features and elaborates on what they *are* and what they can *do*. In addition to making space itself appear, it contributes to the coming into presence of air, earth, and water.

I have not forgotten fire, which is admittedly missing from the list of elements blended with dust. The two principal effects of fire are light and heat, though classical phenomenology has privileged only the first of these to the detriment of the second. How does dust interact with both?

In an effort to respond to this question, we would do well to bring the dust of the *cosmos* back into the fray. Grains of cosmic dust react to radiation in two ways: by scattering and by absorbing it. The scattered portion of radiation is emitted in the form of light, and its absorbed share is converted into "thermal energy," that is, into heat.[2] Astral dust reunites the two effects of fire and propagates the blaze on a cosmic scale. The bouncing of electromagnetic radiation[3] makes space (indeed, the space of space) appear, even as the absorption of radiation's energy veils the appearing.

Narrating the journey of dust through the element of fire and inflating it to cosmic proportions, we come to appreciate the infelicities in the conventional perspective on this substance as something that merely covers up what is of the essence. Fire sheds light on the world, which it hands over to sight (the sun, for the ancients, was nothing but celestial fire), and encrypts itself in heat. Its thermal aspect does not signify the privation of vision in darkness but existence beyond ocular reach. (In another sense, dust shelters that which it covers: extensive glaciers on Mars would have evaporated long ago, were it not for "thick layers of dust protecting the ice."[4]) Although tactile perception is within the purview of phenomenology, vision remains the paramount sense in this school of thought, in line with European Enlightenment and, arguably, with all Western philosophy starting with Plato. Perhaps for this reason, phenomenology has not quite come to terms with the material existence dust epitomizes.

Everything I have written above has been one uninterrupted meditation on the materiality of dust, from how it bridges presumably untraversable distances to how it is embroiled in every elemental domain. This material modality is, no doubt, responsible for the frequent interpretation of our subject matter as obscure and obscuring, a veil that hides from us the hard kernel of reality. And yet, what could be more real or truer than dust? What is more honest than its mute narration of entropy and the styling of space as a plenum, instead of a vacuum? (What does it say about the metaphysical illusions inherent in the act of 'vacuum-cleaning'?) The values of transparency, of the things' unimpeded self-manifestation, of pure light divorced from heat—all these are muddying deceptions, voiced on behalf of clarity and truth. The ordinary conception of dust is subject to distortion by the same metaphysical reversals that have devalued finite life and earthly existence at the expense of the pipe dreams of imperishability. Still, my wager is that, regardless of the residual luggage it carries over from metaphysics, phenomenology might lead us out of the current impasse.

To make space appear in all its materiality before our senses, we must concede that it inevitably shelters dust. This is, in fact, the axiom of space, applicable to the crammed attic of your house, to interstellar expanses, and to everything between these extremes. What it implies for phenomenology is that the seeing and the seen are not the exclusive participants in the "correlation" of vision and that whenever we look at something, we do so through dust. As I have specified, already the ancient Greeks attended to the invisible third, in which they found the conditions of possibility for sight, namely light, or, more broadly, the separation between the seeing and the seen. This third was ideal, ideally transparent, translucent, and, in some respect, transcendent in relation to sensation. With dust, everything changes. Invading the milieu of perception, it vacillates between invisibility and those discrete instances when it appears in the spotlight and immediately redirects our gazes to the space it impregnates. (Dust storms put an end to this vacillation and take visibility away from us, as they clog the air.) It immerses us in immanence, sealing off the gap for transcendent aspirations. And it creates a situation where the seeing and the seen are materially entwined, both because it hails from the bodies of the subject and the object alike and because it hesitates on the threshold between a visible surface and the invisible precondition of sight.

through the dust, darkly

While I was composing the text before you, I was looking on through several layers of dust. There were the specks that had settled on the lenses of my glasses, those that floated in the air between me and my computer monitor, and those resting on that screen. Where was the figure and where the background? How many figures and backgrounds were there? What of the complex interplay between them, a kaleidoscopic rearrangement of focal points in tune with the variations in light, movement, and concentration, dictated by the tiny particles in motion and at rest?

As you are reading this book, you are also gazing at its pages through dust. That is what we share, in addition to the text at hand. "Is that it?" you will ask. "Well, it does not amount to much." But what does the expression "we share dust," or "we have seeing through dust in common," really mean? Does it not suggest that we share materiality and finitude obtruding on everything we do, all the time? Is it not the baseline from which we start, subsequent differences in our perspectives notwithstanding? Doesn't it amount to a great deal?

In everyday life, we act as if no dust existed among us, and between us and the objects we handle. Such insensibility may well be a requisite defense mechanism that authorizes us to go on seeing and living without getting distracted by unintended figures and without being constantly disturbed by the thought of death. Not so when a certain critical mass of dust is reached (and some of us have greater tolerance for the accumulation of this powdery substance than others). In these circumstances, I can no longer afford to turn a blind eye toward it and need to clean my glasses, wipe the computer monitor, and vacuum the room. The fragile balance between visibility and invisibility is then tipped: the status of dust changes from being part of the medium for sight to a seen object. Confusion ensues; as a poet expressed it, "Watching the dust . . . , he lost the things."[5] Having claimed the center of attention, a flagrant and unintended token of past existence excludes from his field of vision the present things themselves. Or, better: the things are lost only to be regained in their disintegration into dusty traces.

Moreover, when dust is deposited in higher concentrations, our relation to it approximates touch, instead of vision, as it further narrows down the distances upon which sight depends. Here, dust cannot be relegated to the unobtrusive background of our existence, for the simple reason that we can no longer see *through* it. The necessary illusion that there are no material interferences with our still unrealized intentions is shattered. To regain mental equilibrium, one is advised to eliminate surplus dust by means of a material negation of materiality. To scrub it out of existence.

Another strategy for tackling this surplus might be more appropriate to the postmetaphysical age. Instead of suppressing the obstinate interferences of matter with our senses, we must learn to see through the dust, darkly. You will have guessed that I am alluding to St. Paul's words in 1 Corinthians 13, "For now we see through a glass, darkly [*en ainigmati*]." To Paul, such dark and flawed vision is a transitory diversion, a birth defect of our fallen nature that will be remedied in the coming perfection of divine salvation. It would not suffice to dust things, illuminating and studying them in minute detail, in order to see clearly. Absent hope, faith, and love, corporeal vision itself is like dust that distorts the true perception of reality. And, again like dust—synonymous not only with the dead but also with the living body and its functions—eyesight ought to be sidelined for the light of authentic and transcendent vision to gush forth.

In Pauline text, the qualifier for today's imperfect way of seeing is *en ainigmati*, "enigmatically." Filtered through retinas, eyeballs, and optic nerves, the world reaches us in a series of "dark riddles" or "obscure sayings" (the literal sense of *enigma*) that hide more than they disclose. Indeed, the enigma of physical sight is akin to that of dust. Both withhold much in the course of presenting themselves and the things that appear around or through them. More precisely, they encrypt the secret right on the surface of appearances. We take their mundane sensory and material reverberations for granted, unless our vision is blurred or there is too much dust to detect what it has enveloped. Paul's radical solution is not to correct these excesses but to do away altogether with the light and warmth of this life, with bodily sight, and with the dusty matter inseparable from the fabric of existence. Such trifles, in Paul's Platonist (or Plotinian) view, pertain to one enigma: the dark and distorted, childish construct of reality we live by. The misconceptions they spawn are inconsequential to those who have received the good news of salvation. With faith as our guide, we should be able to clear our vision of the sand and the dust that matter throws our way, not to speak of the very eyes suited for seeing nothing but the darkness of materiality.

From Paul, I want to borrow the idea of an enigma encoded on the surface of things. It is this enigmatic surface that we caress in any act of dusting. But I certainly do not think that we have any choice other than seeing through the dust, darkly, which is the lesson of the phenomenology I have sketched here. Another Paul, Jean-Paul Sartre, put it somewhat more obliquely when, in a concise 1939 essay on intentionality, he wrote of the "dry dust of the world," "the plain earth, amidst things," which phenomenology simply cannot disregard.[6] In what context does Sartre tie the entire phenomenological tradition to our main theme?

The argument of the French thinker boils down to ineliminable superficiality, of which not even human consciousness is relieved. He begins with the commonsensical (and wrong at that!) account of the relation between consciousness and external reality: "You see this tree, to be sure. But you see it just where it is: at the side of the road, in the midst of the dust, alone and writhing in the heat, eight miles from the Mediterranean coast. It could not enter into your consciousness, for it is not of the same nature as consciousness."[7] On the one hand—the tree, the road, dust, the Mediterranean coast; on the other hand—your consciousness. Except that phenomenology does not endorse the polarization of "external" reality and our "inner" apperception of it. Consciousness has no interiority, if we consider it together with Husserl and Sartre in terms of a vector, or of multiple vectors, tending toward the objects of which it is, in each case, conscious. "If, impossible though it may be, you could enter 'into' a consciousness, you would be seized by a whirlwind and thrown back outside, in the thick of the dust, near the tree, for consciousness has no 'inside'."[8]

The enigma is on the surface: the interiority of consciousness turns inside out, is pulverized, and throws us back into the dust, in which we are and which we are.

"smart dust"

The irreducible presence of dust in space, itself made palpable to us through the multitude of specks that ride the flows of air, offers unique insights into the physicality of experience and the dynamics of cognition. Were we to envision each dust particle as having its own perspective, from a given place it fleetingly occupies, we would have reanimated the Leibnizian notion of God. In Leibniz's philosophy, the mind of God is the sum total of all the conceivable standpoints, materialized in different types of existence from rocks to plants, animals, and humans. Inasmuch as dust amalgamates the vestigial parts of every animate and inanimate being, it comes close to the figuration of Leibniz's God. Other traits speak in favor of this analogy, including the amorphousness of dust and its pervasiveness. Only in one respect does the parallel founder: dust is an "extended," material substance, antithetical to the depersonalized and all-encompassing cognition of God. Or is it?

Researchers from an Orwellian-sounding Institute for Pervasive Computing, based in Zurich, Switzerland, are in a position to expound the applied-technological side of cognizing dust. They promote the concept of "Smart

Dust" (SD) that would "combine sensing, computing, and wireless communication capabilities in an autonomous, dust-grain-sized device." "Dense networks of Smart Dust," Institute member Kay Römer continues, "should then be able to unobtrusively monitor real-world processes with unprecedented quality and scale."[9] Indeed, what better than dust equipped with sensory and communication capabilities could stand for swarm intelligence? What would be off limits, in the face of its "dense networks"? Suggested uses of SD technology include environmental monitoring, scientific observation of animal behavior in natural habitats, and military applications. One does not need much foresight to understand where it could lead us politically. Forget the drone: with Smart Dust, spying would be perfected to such an extent that it could take place *inside* our bodies, when hi-tech dust specks are ingested or inhaled. Total and totalitarian visibility would rule the day.

Sophisticated as it may be, Smart Dust is not quite dust. Not because it excludes organic matter but because it rules out the obscurity, by dint of which the world in and as dust discloses itself. The particles that comprise its dense networks illuminate, register, process, and transmit information about the phenomena they intend to make transparent, the phenomena, with which they have almost nothing in common. In so doing, they drive a wedge between the seeing and the seen, insofar as they stress a dispersed, disembodied gaze that spies on anything that could enter its virtually infinite field of vision, from grazing animals to maneuvering tanks. This is a far cry from Leibniz's God who comprehends the perspective of every single being to the point of coinciding with the totality of their different outlooks. In contrast to Smart Dust, obscurity lingers on, so long as the divine gaze keeps itself occult not by hiding behind or above those through whom it contemplates-creates but by encrypting itself on the surface of their sentient and (apparently) non-sentient material extensions.

The quandaries of Smart Dust aside, this latest collection of gadgets gives us cues as to the mutual imbrication of thinking and being, the mind and the body. Its very name is intriguing, in that it showcases cognition embedded in particles of matter. Trouble is that dust works as a mediator in this embeddedness.

William James, in *The Principles of Psychology*, derisively groups the theories of evolutionary psychologists, convinced of the composite character of mental states, under the heading of "mind-dust." The premise of the thinkers James criticizes is this: "Each atom of the nebula, they suppose, must have had an aboriginal atom of consciousness linked to it; and just as the material atoms have formed bodies and brains by massing themselves together, so the mental atoms, by an analogous process of aggregation, have fused into . . . larger consciousnesses." Consequently, "There must be an infinite number of degrees of consciousness, following the degrees of complication and aggregation of the primordial mind-dust."[10]

James is right to brandish his holistic version of consciousness and its processes before the reductionist evolutionary psychologists of his time, now represented by the British psychologist Nicholas Humphrey, with his theory of "soul dust." The atomic *composition* of reality and of our cogitations is evident solely as a result of its painstaking analytical *de-composition*. Mental and physical atoms are not evident either in the way things show themselves or in the way consciousness receives their self-manifestations. Dust is that which is left over after things have been desiccated and dispersed as time has elapsed, or after our perceptions, sensations, and cognitions have been dissected with the help of methods adapted from natural science. Sitting on a chair, I do not experience its atomic constitution, and, similarly, my memory of this object does not consist of a psychic process subdivided into minute sections that only later, *a posteriori*, assemble to form a coherent whole. The chair is given to me all at once as a support structure for my body (as soon as its parts separate from one another, I will tumble down to the floor) and the same is true for my perception of it.

That said, the attractiveness of the mindset evolutionary psychologists cultivate is undeniable. Fuming against his enemies in *The Principles of Psychology*, James fails to see the charm of their thought: "Atoms of feeling cannot compose higher feelings, any more than atoms of matter can compose physical things! The 'things', for a clear-headed atomistic evolutionist, are not. Nothing is but the everlasting atoms."[11] Precisely! But replace the word "atoms" with "dust," and what do you obtain? Nothing is but dust—of the physical and mental varieties. Spinoza and Leibniz profile existence, including our aspirations, plans, fears and hopes, *sub specie aeternitatis*, under the aspect of eternity. So does Marcel Proust, with his remark that "there is no disgrace great enough to make a man lose heart if he bears in mind that at the end of a certain number of years our buried mistakes will be but invisible dust upon which nature's flowers will smile peacefully."[12] For the very reason that time is ruthless, it is also merciful: sooner or later, it will hand us over to eternity, that is to say, to eternal oblivion. *Sub specie aeternitatis*, from a feigned divine perspective, we see only dust.

Now, what if evolutionary psychologists belong to this venerable tradition, together with Spinoza, Leibniz, and Proust? What if they, like all true materialists, summon us to re-experience reality *sub specie pulveris*, under the aspect of dust, of the dust we, too, will become (and are becoming at this very moment) when what is left of us is aggregated with the grit of the universe? *Sub specie aeternitatis*, thought and being are one, each expressing different ramifications of God's plural existence. Even "dumb" dust is smart. *Sub specie pulveris*, they are also one, welded to finitude by their joint fate of scattering and decomposition. And even "smart" dust is dumb.

Phenomenologically speaking, practical consciousness or intentionality is not atomic, but it is always pulverized, striving concurrently to numerous targets. The stress Heidegger places on a distractedly dispersed way of leading our lives is mindful of the becoming-dust of human concerns. *Zerstreuung*, his word for being-in-the-world, means distraction or dispersion and connotes the state of being scattered or strewn: "Dasein's facticity is such that its being-in-the-world has always dispersed [*zerstreut*] itself or even split itself up [*zersplittert*] into definite ways of being-in. The multiplicity of these is indicated by the following examples: having to do with something, producing something, attending to something and looking after it."[13] Being-in-the-world is being-pulverized.

We constantly morph into dust in everything we do and care for, even and especially as we block out the anxiety awakened by our ultimate, wholesale transformation into dust after death. Trying to evade it, we become dust all the more. As we go toward our destiny, we do not press on by inertia, sleepwalking toward the abyss, but are drawn to the thing from which we desperately attempt to flee. Such is the message of the Middle Eastern fable "Appointment in Samarra," in which a merchant's servant encounters Death at a marketplace in Baghdad and breaks away from it to the city of Samarra so as to hide there. When the merchant confronts Death about the threat it has posed to his servant, the response is: "I did not threaten your servant. It was merely that I was surprised to see him here in Baghdad, for I have an appointment with him tonight in Samarra."[14] And our appointment with dust? It is only a matter of time.

3 ~~BEING~~, DUST, AND TIME

But what god beyond God begins the round
Of dust and time and sleep and agonies?
—JORGE LUIS BORGES, "CHESS"

there *was* something, rather than nothing

As I contemplate dust, it gives me plenty to think about. Before all else, before awakening thought, it furnishes me with the evidence that there is something rather than nothing—or, at least, that there *was* something. It silently yields this testimony to existence from the brink of nonbeing. Where there once was a world, there is now dust, which is a world in its own right.

If I am to believe the philosophers, who, deep down, are expert magicians, the things themselves and even other human beings could be figments of my imagination. But do illusory or ideal beings produce dust? Does a unicorn shed its fur and cutaneous cells, leaving dusty records of itself through bodily renewal and decay? Do the golden-blond hair and fair skin of the Little Prince mingle with the cosmic dust of his faraway planet and with the cells of dried up petals and leaves of his beloved rose? Does the idea of a triangle ever disband into powdery residue?

The answers to these questions are obviously negative. (John Donne proclaims as much in one of his sermons: "And this Vine, and this Rose, and Lilly, and Pomegranats, of Paradise, and this Dew of heaven, are not Dust."[1]) They imply that to secure access to the real, one should not march straight to the things themselves, because that path would only bring us to the cul-de-sac of ideal and ideally dustless entities. Instead, we must circle back to the residues of things, to the material signs of their former existence. The dust that emanates from everything and everyone would, then, serve as a yardstick by which to measure reality, if not as something that is, then as something that once was and that still persists past its term. It would puncture the hot-air balloon of perfection. And it would mend the divide between animate and inanimate beings, whose remains are interspersed with one another, and contrast both to imaginary, ideal entities that do not (cannot) generate dust. (God addresses his own regret of being dustless by creating the world and, specifically, Adam and Eve, through whom he became dust vicariously, well in advance of Jesus's incarnation.) Wallace Stevens outlines the interface of reality with dust, when he denies "the premise that reality/Is a solid," conjecturing instead that "it may be a shade that traverses/A dust, a force that traverses a shade."² Doubly vanishing, reality is a trace left on a trace, a shadow cast upon dust. Assuming that Stevens has in mind Horace's words, *Pulvis et umbra sumus* ("We are but dust and shadow"), the reality he is hinting at is what or who we ourselves are: the *sumus* of *The Odes* (IV.vii.16).

What is more, the evidence dust offers is of a temporal nature. It commemorates the time when the entities, whose particles have entered it, were still coherent and whole. But, since finite material existence precludes perfect coherence and wholeness, since, outside the straightjacket of metaphysics, being entails unremitting flux, growth, decay, and metamorphosis, one cannot say with any degree of certainty whether the "origins" of dusty remains carry on as this human, this book, this tree, this table, this dog, or whether they have been transmogrified into dust *tout court*. Was the slow process of disintegration that culminated in this particular dust ball a part of their regeneration (in the case of living beings) and their daily depreciation (in the case of inanimate objects), or did it affect any or all of them in their totality? Did the dog die and was the book burned? Did anything other than their dispersed particles remain, after they participated in the universal proliferation of dust? The evidentiary power we have praised does not extend to these queries.

Be this as it may, the potential of dust is not to be underestimated. In addition to letting space appear for a blazing instant illuminated by a ray of light, it warrants a tangible and, indeed, spatial appearance of time. Apart from insinuating that there *was* something, it also indicates that enough time has elapsed for hair, fur, and dead skin to be shed, for pollen to fly off a tree, for a dying star to be pulverized, or for industrial pollutants, containing silicon, aluminum, calcium, and dozens of toxins, to form copious clouds. Dust measures the lifetimes of animate and inanimate beings and processes, even if it desists from stamping existence with expiration dates and, thus, indefinitely defers the final moment of vanishing. A spatial gauge of time, it plays the role of what Jacques Derrida christens *différance*: the simultaneous spatialization of time and temporalization of space.

In retrospect, dust chronicles both the gradual break up of beings and how they get a second lease on life, the opportunity to lead a posthumous existence in a random recombination of their remains. If there were a god of dust, the "god beyond God" Borges invokes,[3] then it would most likely be Hindu Śiva-the-Destroyer. Lest we be misled by his terrible attributes, Śiva is not an external annihilating force; he is the temporal gist of finite beings, whose gradual or rapid manner of passing away is, at bottom, what they are. His actions uphold the living order, which needs change, dying away and rejuvenation. And, last but not least, he destroys death or puts an end to the misconception that death is the end of existence, just as dust teaches us about the afterlife of its sources in the contingent communities they establish.

The work of time and of Śiva, whose native element is fire, is to pulverize composite beings, sparing neither you, nor me, nor anything around us. Time is like a shredding machine, uninterruptedly spitting out dust. The finer the particles come out, the more efficiently the machine performs, the more homogenous the remains, and the more the trace is produced as already erased, its origins scarcely legible. Let us not hurry, nevertheless, to conjure up the phantasm of time as a gigantic grinder, devouring beings that are, in any event, never exempt from its influence. Each of us, together with this notebook, this pen, and this coat, is a temporal shredding machine that has its idiosyncratic mode of falling apart and that, for the time being, holds itself together, even as some particles abandon it and merge with those generated by other self-shredders. Each of us is, in other words, a miniature dust-yielding factory in the warehouse of existence.

It follows (and this thought veers toward deconstruction) that to give time is to let a thing be in keeping with the kind of fragmentation and decay appropriate to it. Giving time is allowing something or someone to tread their singular path of turning into dust. In lieu of the ancient desire to save the ephemeral and inconstant actuality from corruption and decay, the love of finite beings in their finitude demands that we bestow on them the right to be converted into dust in their due time and in their own style. Not to be misjudged as a coldly detached, indifferent, or nihilistic posture, this demand is a loving exhortation. Only those who are, themselves, on the dusty road of becoming-dust can love others who (or that) have embarked on a similar journey at birth or at the time of their fabrication. Which means that the focus on dust is more than a melancholy presentiment of doom, a Romantic lament over the ruins and the tombs, or the arresting horror we sense in Walter Benjamin's take on *Angelus Novus* who watches the raging storm of debris that is world history. After all, love involves fecundity, which brings us the tidings of the future, promising or not.

the generation of dust

For Aristotle, the power of generativity, the capacity to originate another one like you, is the prerogative of living beings and of nature (*phusis*) in general that distinguishes them from artifacts, the products of *technē*. Yet, again, dust wreaks havoc in this neat conceptual distinction. Animate and inanimate beings generate dust, tirelessly giving birth to "dry rot," and, therefore, feeding the premonition of death ever since the moment of their emergence.

Broadly understood as synonymous with dust, "dry rot" is not my expression. It is a speck of meaning that has flown in my direction from Joseph Brodsky's astute observation: "The core of things is dry rot. . . ./Dust. When you switch lights on,/there's nothing but dust to see./That's true even if the thing/is sealed up hermetically."[4] Instead of being born from the depths of beings, dust egresses from their exteriority, the surface, which is not very different from their "core." (We are back to the superficial enigmas of the previous chapter.) Nor is it the case that the living gush forth from the inside out, while inanimate objects breed waste through physical friction on the outside. Akin to consciousness bereft of interiority, the body is also all skin, an exteriority folded upon itself, as Jean-Luc Nancy, among others, underlines. So, where does my idea of depth come from, if not from the superimposition of many superficies made of dust, a thousand dusty plateaus? It takes time for the dry rot of "core" layers to be liberated, or for future entropy to pass over into the present. But when this finally happens, the entropic movement will not have the last word. Dust is the outcome of degeneration, which is, also, the generation of refuse, and thus a positive, fecund, productive development. Not the work of mourning but the pledge of a new birth.

The first humans are fashioned out of dust, whence in the aftermath of the original sin they are bound to return. Dust is the womb of the sixth day of Creation and the tomb of fallen humanity. How to interpret the phrase "dust thou art," avoiding its demotion to a cliché? It suggests that you have your origin outside yourself: banally, in the Creator who breathed life into your nostrils, and, less so, in what existed, lived, and disintegrated before you. The divine act is not *creatio ex nihilo*; it recycles past matter in the figure of the human. In plain terms, the phrase intimates that you are what has been!

Made of dust, Adam and Eve are dust's next generation. Along with their descendants, they (we) will generate still more dust in previously unseen quantities, ample enough to blanket the blue planet twice over, through their (our) "industries." Sharing God's attraction to dust (which, *mutatis mutandis*, is our attraction to ourselves), we nonetheless produce dust of an uninspired, dead, and deadening variety—one that chokes life and induces disease, such as pneumoconiosis, attributable to the inhalation of asbestos or of coal dust. The second part of the curse, ". . . and unto dust shalt thou return," describes something more sinister than the reinstatement of cosmic balance and the odyssey of matter upon the completion of its human detour back to the primordial elements. With historical hindsight, the curse broaches the issue of de-creation, the diabolical power of humanity to drag the rest of its planetary home along with itself into dust.

The returns *of* dust and *to* dust set a temporal rhythm for finite existence. Even if the shift of prepositions from "of" to "to" declares a change of aspect, rather than of substance, it makes a tremendous difference. From receiving dust, mostly with hostility, we pass to a state of being received by it. Between "of" and "to"—an entire lifetime. Everything that, and everyone who, has ever been, returns in the shapeless shape of dust, which conserves something of the departed.

Besides serving as a sign for the destruction of the past and for the surviving remnants in the present, dust betokens the future. Brazilian author Clarice Lispector encapsulated the generativity of dust with the characteristic acumen of her writings, calling it "*a filha das coisas*," "the daughter of things."[5] She meant to say with this expression that things are productive or re-productive, they work at creating their ghosts, morsels of matter that used to comprise them and are now devoid of form. Dust is the things' next generation, their mode of surviving, achieved at the cost of their identities and identifiable outlines. Such family ties are everywhere: matter is the mother of dust-the-daughter, and history is the web of filiation between the past of things and the future of their nebulous remains. As it elapses, time works on matter, loves it, couples with it, so that the daughter would be born. Dry rot is in the core of things, fertilized by temporality as soon as they are brought into being. No wonder that sealing a thing hermetically does not safeguard it from becoming-dust! What nests in its shallow interiority is the time that overflows the static order of spatiality. Dust is this excess of time over space. (This provisional definition also befits existence in general.)

Nor does keeping a house under lock and key, uninhabited and untouched, stop the buildup of "dry rot." There, dust celebrates the Sabbath of things. Covering them, it signals that they are resting, having been extracted from the context of unremitting use. A mundane miracle, it returns the things it envelops back to their virginal state. And, in the same breath, it reports on the work done on and with things in the absence of a human user—the work of time, fraying them in accordance with the becoming-threadbare of the world.

On a galactic scale, dust itself is generative, insofar as it provides the building blocks for the formation of planets, stars, and asteroids.[6] Discharged from supernovas, or stellar explosions that fleetingly compete in brilliance with the glow of an entire galaxy, cosmic dust first condenses from the gases that have vaporized everything in their vicinity. In the second stage of the celestial bodies' production, clouds of dust cool the supernova further and transform it into more dust, primed to serve as construction material for celestial bodies.[7] Along with mortal humans, albeit at a different pace, entire planets come from and return to dust. Passive and active, generated and generating, dust amalgamates both beings and times—the past, the present, and the future—in a substance that is not one and that is perpetually ready to recommence the circle of becoming when hope seems to have died.

an image of eternity

In *Timaeus*, Plato's designation for time is *eikō . . . kineton tina aiōnos*, "a moving image of eternity" (37d). Eternal are the Ideas, unaffected by empirical accidents of the physical realm, immune to the fluxes of becoming and destruction. How does time reflect these non-worldly realities? By moving in a circle in the case of celestial bodies and the World Soul, and thus partaking in the eidetic sphere. The completion of a circle, which has neither a beginning nor an end, mirrors the perfection of Ideas that are not generated and do not degenerate. The moving image of eternity is the timeless time of being that has spurned becoming, the being sundered from nothing.

Dust, as we have already seen, is incompatible with Ideas and ideals. Inscribed in the logic of becoming, it augurs the crumbling of things as much as their renewal. If accidents here-below leave Plato's true beings unaffected, then dust does not register at all on the radars of ideality. It is an accident of the accident, a fugacious shadow of the superfluous, a transient next-to-nothing. Unless. . . .

The first crack in the argument develops once we think back to the circular movement of dust, with all its turns and returns. It sends us back to the rotation of a non-homogeneous substance, wherein things experience entropy and receive their chance at a posthumous rebirth. From cosmic dust to the Biblical *humus*, it both antecedes and succeeds the generation of beings, staying as unaffected by their comings and goings as the Ideas themselves. *Sub specie aeternitatis*—a perspective, which is, paradoxically, also *sub specie pulveris*—the daughter of things is actually their mother and, therefore, its own grandmother and grandchild.

The second crack forms when we supplement the evanescence of dust with its resilience. Evincing the destruction of past existence, it testifies to the staying power of something (matter?) that obdurately persisted outside the constraints of form. Dust has the air of destructible indestructability, which is a circuitous way to say *time*. It signals the *necessity of the accident*, the inexorable force of becoming, suspended between being and nothing, but a force that, itself, does not become. A gentle refusal of complete evanescence, a protest, lodged at the heart of mortality, against the finality of death, dust is the image of eternity stamped on every least bit of material reality. It is the point where the vectors of frailty and tenaciousness intersect, attesting to a strength that is not equivalent to stubborn immutability.

The third crack is in our realization that dust transgresses the boundaries between temporal modalities. Dust is at home in non-linear, non-sequential time; everything obtains in it all at once, in the babel of the past, the present, and the future. Such synchronicity borders on spatiality (as Immanuel Kant sees it in his first *Critique*), which makes sense to those who recall that dust is spatialized time and temporalized space. Eternal being, if there is one, does not endure in a never-ending *now*, but comprises this very mélange of what is, has been, and will ever be. Eternity is time configured as space, or space indistinguishable from time, and dust is its swirling, rolling, disintegrating, and conglomerating image.

Dust and eternity are irreconcilable, provided that we still cling to a strict separation between being and becoming. But a rift between these two realms is unnecessary and downright harmful. Nietzsche, for one, knew full well that one of the hardest and most decisive challenges for philosophy recovering from the protracted nightmare of metaphysics was that of (literally) squaring the circle, or coordinating the inflexibility of being with the volatility of becoming. He summed up his solution in the doctrine of "the eternal recurrence of the same," with the affirmation of what transpired in each second of a life and consent to relive everything an infinite number of times precisely as it came to pass. The imagery is evocative: "The eternal hourglass of existence is turned over again and again, and you with it, speck of dust."[8] The ephemeral dust that we are is *contained* in the form of existence, urging our becomings to be replayed over and over. This form is being, construed as a dynamic process of repetition, not as a static structure. The hourglass is empty and pointless without the specks enclosed in it; the dust of existence is senseless without the form that receives it. Eternity, the recurrent turning of a rudimentary clock, includes in itself the wearing on of time, which, for its part, is measured in units of dust, the dust that we are.

The knot of being and time is glaring when entities are reduced to crumbly residue. Just as the infinitesimal pieces of planets, animals, plants, humans, and inanimate objects coalesce with one another in dust, so their asynchronous temporal rhythms undergo a kind of fusion there. And yet, it would be precipitous to trumpet the victory of ontological and chronological non-differentiation. The dust of existence is beholden to singularity, to the extent that, within the framework of the eternal recurrence, it reiterates the minutest details in the life of each one. The singular also endures in actual balls of dust, those aleatory conjunctions that can, at any time, crumble, thus restituting individuality and independence, disparate existential rhythms and ways of being, to their components. The already dead cells and microscopic fibers of paper may keep on rotting, even as pollen grains may reach the flowers they are destined to fertilize or continue their peregrinations on the wings of insects or the wind. Sub-individual singularity is not lost here.

The eternity we are pursuing in the dust is not the boringly endless and uneventful stagnation of perfect being but the form of change that fits mutable phenomena like a glove. In it, in this form, dust has not settled, because the hourglass keeps on turning, incessantly. Nothing could be further from the eternal recurrence of the same, which, thanks to the returns of difference and of dust, harmonizes agility with the suspension of activity, than the perpetual peace of the cemeteries. (Thus, Nietzsche bypasses Kant and reconnects with the Aristotelian "energy of rest," peculiar to the "unmoved mover.") When dust flies, a period of intense agitation is underway; when it settles, a stage of repose begins. Normally, we experience the alternation of commotion and tranquility, for example, in the diurnal cycles, also known as the circadian rhythms. The hourglass of eternal recurrence, however, exceeds the immediacy of biological and psychic life, which it does not negate. The other and the same, difference and repetition, movement and rest, coexist in it not as mutually exclusive phases taking place in succession but as the content and the form of a single process-state. Whether it flies or settles down, dust is the index of this strange repose in agitation. The turning of Nietzsche's sand clock (or dust clock, if you will) does not stipulate that eternity should cancel time out. It affirms finite temporalities of all kinds with every return, at every turn.

But what if the *locus* of the sovereign decision on the affirmation or negation of existence were not the existing subject? What if eternity itself were fed up with us, as Palestinian poet Mahmoud Darwish fears: "My eternity is fed up with me,/and my tomorrow/is sitting on my chair/like a crown of dust."[9] For Darwish, dust is much more than a measure of time. It represents the crowning moment of the moment, regal yet primed for dilapidation, together with "me." Allied to eternity, dust reigns over being and time, and gives the lie to the human presumption of power and control. The royal accouterments of dust multiply when Abel is anointed "king on the throne of dust,"[10] an expression that keeps cropping up in Darwish's writings, for instance with reference to the limits of language: "With a word without meaning, interpretation makes you a king on a throne of dust."[11] How dust invests and undermines human sovereignty is another story altogether, one that has to do with the overactive immune systems of our bodies and with our ambivalent relation to the past.

4 ALLERGIC REACTIONS

Dust in the air suspended
Marks the place where a story ended.
Dust inbreathed was a house—
The walls, the wainscot and the mouse,
The death of hope and despair,
This is the death of air.

—T. S. ELIOT, "LITTLE GIDDING"

"foreign work"

Across the American Southwest, dust has become lethal. Valley fever, an oft-times chronic disease caused by the airborne fungi *Coccidioides immitis* and *Coccidioides posadasii*, is contracted by inhaling the dust that blows from the construction sites, dumping grounds, and deserts of Arizona, California, Nevada, New Mexico, and Texas. In the most severe cases, fungi-laced particles infect, besides the patients' lungs and respiratory system, their bone marrow and the brain. One breath can result in a lifetime of suffering and death.

Valley fever is a stark reminder about the qualities of dust, which, seemingly innocuous and domesticated, is a latent threat pervading the environment outside the confines of the household it is usually associated with. It proves beyond a shadow of doubt that, for all its unremarkable nature, dust cannot be tamed, contained, made familiar or familial.

The repercussions of dust allergies are not as dramatic as those of valley fever, but they likewise obey the principle of something inconspicuous suddenly turning dangerous and potentially incapacitating. In each case, it is a living element of dust that functions as a trigger, be it fungus, pollen, or dust mites. Passing below the thresholds of sense perception, microscopic life invades us from within and either infects our bodies or provokes a disproportionate immune response, more harmful to the organism than the entity from which it tries to defend itself. Allergies are the biological alarms that sound when the boundary between the inside and the outside is breached. They afflict us when our bodies distinguish, at a non-cognitive level, the other as other, as an invader, alien to the organism it assaults.

Yet, things are more knotty than that. Consider that our bodies are not autonomous units sealed off from other living creatures and from our natural or constructed environments. Home to untold varieties of bacteria, some of them beneficial for the proper workings of the digestive tract and other organs, the human body is more of an ecosystem with human and nonhuman participants than a castle under our sovereign possession and vigilant protection. Before we are born and time and again after birth, we let the outside in, not in violation of our integrity but by way of making life possible. It is increasingly difficult to say who "the other" and "the self" are in the complex community of human genetic materials and nonhuman inhabitants that comprise us.

I am not arguing that the difference between the same (or the self) and the other is totally irrelevant and that, therefore, immune defenses against viruses, harmful bacteria, and other intruders are unnecessary. Even if it were practically realizable, unconditional hospitality would have been incongruous with life, which requires certain limits and margins for its flourishing, variable and membrane-like as they may be. The *unconditional* hospitality of a biological cell to water, for instance, would, after awhile, cause the cell's walls to burst. Unconditionally, only the same can welcome the same.

How would things change if the dwelling where I receive the other were not surrounded by walls, fences, and concrete barriers but were delimited by a breathable membrane? Don't our bodies experience dust allergies because they forget that they are separated from the outside by membranes, rather than walls, and over-react to harmless substances that traverse their porous boundaries? When allergens are encountered in the mucous portions of our nostrils, eyes, ears, or corners of the mouth, their proteins receive the markers "foreign" and "dangerous" from our immune systems. But, much like in our sociopolitical systems, foreignness need not automatically flash a bright-red "Danger!" sign before our eyes. Justified with regard to valley fever, the transition from the first marker to the second is specious when it comes to dust (and many other kinds of) allergies.

Actually, foreignness is one of the semantic components in the term *allergy*, which conjoins the Greek words *allos* (foreign, other) and *ergon* (work or act). Without being innately dangerous, a foreign body puts something to work, activates or enacts something. This "something" refers to the body's own defenses, from the standpoint of which an allergen seems threatening. In other words, our immune system is set to work by the other, by a foreign element, which is, as I have mentioned, less perilous to our well-being than the immune reaction it elicits. Derrida has written a fair bit on the self-undermining logic of autoimmunity (particularly in *Rogues*[1]) and what it holds in store for communities, political and not only. But we have to be more precise than such a generalization would allow. Autoimmune diseases and reactions vary, as do allergic response. So, what is unique about dust allergies?

Three out of the five most common allergens are present in dust: mold, pollen, and mites. This, I submit, is not a meaningless factoid, but an illustration of a cogent argumentative point. If dust induces so many allergies, so frequently, that is due to its extreme foreignness, even to itself. A haphazard assemblage of arbitrary materials, it does not boast an inherent identity. Dust is truly other inasmuch as it is other to itself. (To be more accurate yet, there isn't an "itself" of dust to speak of.) It is pre-dispersed in its very gathering. At the risk of sounding tautological, I should note that dust allergies are allergies *to* dust and, in a broader sense, to a dispersed other or others, if not to dispersion as such. All in all, in dust, the boundaries are *always already* crossed between the domestic sphere and the cosmos, between different species and biological kingdoms, between frazzles of artifice and byproducts of plants, animals, and humans. What, then, intrudes into our bodies together with dust particles is intrusion itself; what disconcerts our defenses is disconcert itself; what receives the molecular label "other" is otherness itself. Allergies to dust are meta-allergies to foreignness *as* foreignness, to a loose grouping that is aleatory (accidental) and is not bound by any inner connections.

In the sixties and seventies of the last century, Derrida took one of his mentors, Emmanuel Levinas, to task for thinking of another human being as wholly other. He pointed out this puzzle: a human other is both more and less other to me than an inanimate thing. More, because—unlike a physical object I can study with the help of chemistry, physics, and related sciences, and thus acquire satisfactory knowledge of—another human being is inexhaustible and inaccessible insofar as I cannot get "under her skin" and approach the world entirely from her point of view. Less, because, formally, another human being is, like myself, human.[2]

We could linger in this irresolvable contradiction, as Derrida prefers to do, or we could observe that, in dust, another human is wholly other, including to herself. Be this as it may, in the metaphysical history of the West, obdurate otherness has been a powerful stimulus for allergic reactions. In an influential essay, "The Trace of the Other," Levinas writes: "From its infancy philosophy has been struck with a horror of the other that remains other—with an insurmountable allergy."[3] Sounds like the French philosopher is talking about what we've dubbed "meta-allergies," activated through foreign work (*allos ergon*) by the pulverization of identity! The trace of the other is dusty.

out of place

To be perfectly honest, I, myself, suffer from acute pollen and dust allergies. As I relate in *Through Vegetal Being*, a book I wrote together with Luce Irigaray,

> Just when the revival of spring happens and plants begin to bristle with their radiant colors, I find myself cut off from the outside, barely able to see, smell, taste, or breathe. A watery barrier arises between my sense organs and their corresponding objects, disrupting the transparent workings of intentionality. Our physical and spiritual alienation from plants is, in the end, one and the same as our alienation from the rest of the organic and inorganic universe.[4]

Dust allergies display a similar pattern, governed by our estrangement from material reality, rife with gritty fractions of things. Which is why I try to undo in thinking and in writing the allergic responses of my body to the flowering and grinding-down of the world.

Allergies do not stop at mere physiological reactions to outside irritants; they are the offshoots of collective thought processes, reaching far back in historical time and structuring our lives in the present. Together with the frenzied sterilization of our lived environments, massive pollution, which has not left any element on, in, and around the earth unscathed, accounts for the prevalence of allergies in industrial and postindustrial modernity.[5] By dint of the extremes of pollution and sterilization, we are particularly out of sync with life, and even such primary life-processes as eating or breathing become problematic. Allergic reactions are misplaced, in that they conflate otherness with danger, and they cause us to be out of place in our homes, on the streets, in the woods, in the fields, in the midst of life.

Out-of-placeness is a pivotal, if rarely acknowledged, trait of the human. Exacerbated in late modernity, it haunts everything we take to be typical of humanity. Ontological dislocation does not begin in this era, of course; it is coeval with the anthropic mission as such. The one entrusted with apportioning to each being its meaning is bereft of a legitimate place *within* the network of assignments. The expulsion precipitated by our purported sovereignty passes for the greatest privilege or the highest, most sublime station. With time the gap between the expelled and the dominated widens: more and more, humans experience the disarticulation, maladjustment, or lack of fit between ourselves and the world—a situation that drives us, and the world, toward an irreparable disaster. The only standpoint we are willing to hold fast is that of nothing: "pure" consciousness, abstract cogitation, awareness of the impending death. . . . Then, from this non-place, from this unsettling sense of out-of-placeness, we proceed to appropriate every single place under the sky, including the minerals, plants, and animals that make it *their* home.

Bluntly put, we delude ourselves by thinking that we are fragments of spirit, thrust by a tragic error into the material sphere, to which we do not belong. But there is something else that has no footing in the matrix of the real. When, in nineteenth-century English, the word *dust* still referred to garbage, it was categorized as "matter out of place,"[6] an expression Mary Douglas attributes to Lord Chesterfield (1694–1773), renowned for the letters he wrote to his son "on manners and morals." Philosophers have been clinging to a comparable notion for much longer. With Gnostic maximalism that equates materiality and evil, they have deemed *all* matter to be out of place to the extent that it disrupts the neatness and sterility of spirit. For them, all matter is dust (or, perhaps, garbage). This perverse intuition is one of the triggers for the metaphysical allergy that has afflicted Western philosophy since time immemorial.

We are now ready to rethink dust allergies along the following lines: they are the *misplaced reactions of spirit out of place to matter out of place.* True: spirit and matter are polarized and bitterly opposed to one another in this scheme of things. Their opposition should not, however, detract us from an underlying similarity, namely that humans and dust share the quality of out-of-placeness. So versatile, light, and errant is dust that it cannot be nailed down to a spot where it would incontrovertibly belong in the orders of intellection, of the universe, or of the house. So mimetically inclined (prone to imitating other creatures), indeterminate, and rootless are humans that it is impossible to define them within a fixed realm of being. The parallels are suggestive enough to indicate that, in its allergy to matter figured as dust, spirit reacts to a disconcerting aspect of itself. At any rate, out-of-placeness turns out to be the elusive shared groundwork of the ideal and the real, spirit and matter, humanity and dust. Read against the grain, the Biblical "Dust thou art . . ." enables the recognition of each participant in these dyads in the other and holds the key to overcoming metaphysical dust allergies that have been suffocating the planet and ourselves.

As we discovered in Chapter 1, the daily fight against dust on the invisible domestic front is fated to displace and redistribute rather than eliminate it. But to displace "matter out of place" is to obey its own anarchic directive! We labor under the misconception that, in the course of cleaning or dusting, we expel the undesirable from the dwelling and, with this sweepingly decisive gesture, reassert the law of the house, its economy. We work to prevent the "foreign work" of allergic reaction. Yet, foreign to itself, dust has already challenged and enervated our designs from the get-go. (The war on dust, a hallmark of modern hygiene, reverberates with the political hygiene of the war on terror. The fight against terrorism similarly dislocates the almost undetectable and eminently mobile political phenomenon it combats from one hotspot to another, escalating destruction and hatred along its meandering way.)

No means are spared, no chemicals and detergents left untouched, for the sake of making the household workable, though, perhaps, not livable. In the microcosm of the private dwelling and in our social macrocosm alike, ecological apprehensions pale in comparison with the economic ones. Dusting and cleaning are stripped of their environmental sensibility and dispense more pollution than protection or care. Allergies are more debilitating when chemical agents, as ubiquitous as dust, surround us and penetrate our bodies. The innermost places of our existence are, themselves, out of place, that is to say, out of tune with life.

eating our dust . . .

Not by accident, two of the most thought-provoking and relatively recent books on dust—Joseph Amato's 2000 *Dust: A History of the Small & the Invisible* and Carolyn Steedman's 2001 *Dust: The Archive and Cultural History*—contemplate a variety of ways, in which this stuff can make us sick. Dust is the generally invisible wellspring of infections, industrial air pollution, and the all-too-literal archive fever that can lead a scholar, exposed to the crumbling leather of book bindings, to develop migraine headaches or to break out in hives. The Great Cleanup, initiated in the nineteenth century, did nothing to stop the onslaught of dust. "As dust and dirt are banished," Amato admits, "waste and garbage multiply."[7]

By now, we are well acquainted with the bewildering logic of dust, according to which "less" means "more." Having said that, a physical or physiological sickness associated with it is a symptom of still another malady. One of the reasons why dust allergies afflict us in our houses is that we have no idea of what it means to dwell; we are out of practice as far as dwelling is concerned. Take mobility, for instance. An increase in traffic on our streets and highways leads to an upsurge of road dust, raised by the speeding vehicles. Paved road dust is not an abstract atmospheric pollutant, but one that substantially augments the incidence of allergies. In 1999, researchers from California found that, in addition to the toxic stew of exhaust, tire, and break lining wear particles, this kind of dust contained allergens from twenty other sources, including pollen, animal dander, and mold.[8] Lifted by the passing traffic, this mix hovers over the road and heightens the concentration of allergens in the vicinity. "Dust allergies" are not circumscribed to domestic problems alone. They make the difference between the inside and the outside of the dwelling hazy and they are aggravated by our collective propensity to raise dust on the highway or at the factory, on a construction site or at a farm.

Kicking inordinate quantities of road dust into the air, our mobility is part and parcel of the restlessness factored into the modern condition. The aspirations of progress set off an unforgiving race to outdo other individuals, countries, generations. The motto of a modern individual boils down to the crude idiomatic expression, "Eat my dust!" But, since dust does not respect oppositional pairings, our victory in this mad race is equivalent to defeat. After we surpassed a critical mass of dust generated by industrial-scale activities, we have outpaced ourselves and exceeded the limits of what our bodies can tolerate. Today, we eat our own dust. The spike in allergies, asthmas, and other chronic conditions is, at once, a medal in this race without a clear finish line and a sign of our defeat.

If dwelling means remaining, staying in place, or abiding, then it sharply contrasts with restlessness, which instigates our wanderings from place to place and underpins our dissatisfaction with any given locale. When the byproducts of our restless pursuits invade our houses in the form of dust, they make our dwellings nearly uninhabitable. By disturbing and depleting topsoil through construction and intensive agriculture, we interfere with the stability of the earth, which is the substratum of our lives, forcing its upper layers, together with the molds and fungi they contain, into the air. Dust storms—notably, the 1930s Dust Bowl in the US Great Plains and the Canadian Prairies—are the outcomes of this process. So is valley fever, most common "among agricultural workers and construction crews."[9] In a thoroughly mobile and mobilizing order, which uproots human populations, nonhuman animals and plants, and even the earth itself, staying in place is an exception. The dust allergies we suffer in our homes bear witness to the eclipse of dwelling in an age of global unrest.

If, however, to dwell is also to inhabit actively, then the picture we have painted thus far is somewhat wanting. According to Heidegger, dwelling, in the Old English and High German sense of *bauen*, hinges on building and cultivation, edifying and letting-grow.[10] Both of these endeavors obligate us to excavate, furrow, upturn, and otherwise break the ground that would sustain new architectural constructions and agricultural projects. To Heidegger's insight we might add the observation that, more and more, building predominates over cultivation. We do not *let* plants and animals grow; we *make* them grow, and (genetic or environmental) engineering serves as a model for our dealings with what we used to call *nature*. Accomplishing the forever-incomplete "home work" of dwelling, we must involuntarily generate dust and assume responsibility for the "foreign work" of the allergies it foments. By implication, we forget dwelling not by embarking on an endless road trip, but by inhabiting our planetary home with mad intensity and ecstatic abandon, building and farming on and on. We dig, bore into the earth, suffuse the air with it, and, presiding over this *coitus* of the elements, churn up tons of dust. "This is the death of air," T. S. Eliot would quip—and of many other things besides air. We consign to oblivion the dwellings we construct or cultivate in the very process of their construction or cultivation. Shrouded in the clouds of dust our activities emit is the question *why?*

that has egged these activities on in the first place. Despite its provenance from the desire to feel at home in the world, the work of dwelling is yoked to extraneous purposes. So long as economic growth trumps all other considerations, housing and produce, to which building and cultivation are reduced, will be akin to dust—a more or less unintended consequence of our incorrigible unrest.

The tired antithesis of nature and culture collapses under the weight of dwelling, charged with the tasks of building and cultivating. Among other places, its collapse is felt in dust, consisting of industrial, cosmic-elemental, and biological components. As for the dwelling rooted in restlessness (*viz.*, in human uprooting), it propagates all three varieties in a concoction of toxic chemicals, disturbed topsoil along with the mold spores that reproduce there, farmed animals' dander and plant pollen, not to mention the erosion of our mass-produced and mass-consumed reality. Proliferating at the behest of the current economic system, with its insatiable appetite for "growth," the excess of matter, combined with the incessant movement that agitates it, yields a surplus of dust— a faithful but uncredited companion of surplus value. These overwhelming dusty traces redouble today's phenomena that, not yet ground to dust, impinge on our hyper-stimulated senses and overstretched attentive concentration spans. At the level of our immune and nervous systems, we eat our dust. The allergies of the twenty-first century may not be reactions to foreignness but, alternatively, to the colossal footprint of our oblivious dwelling, incommensurate with life itself.

5 A COMMUNITY OF REMNANTS

Without a single word
the essence is conveyed.

. . .

It is dust in timeless open space,
is flowing, foaming sea spume,
shallow or deep, cohering, dispersing.
One out of a thousand contains all thousand.

—SIKONG TU, "THE IMPLICIT STYLE"

{{*Communal configurations*:

1 Dust balls are tangles. They accrete around the infrastructure of a few hairs, furs, or strands of cloth. A momentary concentration.

2 Dust clouds are dispersed, atmospheric events. One could say: diasporic. A spreading, creeping saturation.

3 Layers of dust are leveled, even, democratic, egalitarian. They "paint their gray on gray." Repose, also momentary, combined with the feeling of a steady descent into nothing.}}

{{The word *dust* is already a community of meanings, bringing together, outside the constraints of essential unity, a noun and a verb, moistness and dryness, the cosmos and a studio apartment.}}

{{In dust, as dust, we are thrown together, wasted together, with plant and animal matter, the cutaneous cells of others, minerals, cosmic debris, threads of clothing, and so on. Where does this desultory assemblage begin, and where does it end?}}

{{*With a wink to Kant.* Dusty communities spring up through the combination of two factors:

1 The intermingling of snippets of skin, fabric, book binding, burned meteorite particles, etc.

2 Overlapping cycles of renewal and/or decay in human, animal, and vegetal traces, combined with the entropy of inorganic entities—indeed, of the entire universe.

These are the spatial and temporal conditions of possibility for (domestic) dust. A transcendental aesthetic of dust is awaiting our elaboration.}}

{{Nothing and no one joins the community of dust intentionally, owing to an act of volition. We, together with everything and everyone that is, are heaped into it. As dust gathers, parts of us are gathered into it, until, one day, the entire body is claimed. In the words of Shelley: "First, our pleasures die—and then/Our hopes, and then our fears—and when/These are dead, the debt is due,/Dust claims dust—and we die too."[1]}}

{{Pause on the ties that bind dusty communities. Usually, relations are the idealized connections between things. I am here, as is my dog, but where is the relation between us? Or, between this pen and this paper? Or, between my fingertips and computer keys? Spatial articulations are, no doubt, less abstract but they still skirt the question where the relation itself resides. Dust, on the other hand, *is* the relation between the hair, and the pollen, and grains of sand. The meaning of each "component" is re-contextualized as soon as they are admitted into the ephemeral community of dust. There is no dust, absent the makeshift nexus of hair, pollen, and grains of sand that, in its midst, have let go of their identities.}}

{{As I write books, I occasionally cut sentence fragments, sentences, or even entire paragraphs and paste them to a separate file titled "Scraps," "Rests," or "Remnants." I sometimes revisit these depositories containing the dust of thought. Discarded, ideas commune noiselessly there, as do the particles of dust in physical space.}}

{{How does dust come into the world? (This question is a semantic palindrome that also asks: How does the world come—dissolve—into dust?)

1 Through cosmic events, such as violent star explosions

2 When living beings and inanimate entities shed small pieces of themselves

3 Thanks to strong winds disturbing loose soil, lifting fine particulate matter into the air

4 When speeding vehicles take over the role of wind gusts

5 Through industrial pollution

6 By means of pulverization, in time.

Decay, splitting, and division of matter into tiny units are matter's self-affirmation and profusion. Dust is the aftermath of a prior unity; traces are always dusty (see Chapter 4), but dust itself is a trace. Separated from their diverse sources, the elements of dust do not appear in isolation from one another. On the contrary, they constitute an ensemble within their new context, while remaining unincorporated into a larger whole (there isn't really a "whole" to speak of). Dust is the precarious hanging-together of remnants, particles, fragments. It is the community that survives after an organic unity has faded away.}}

{{Dust *qua* conglomeration and dispersion: 1) conglomeration of the conglomerated; 2) conglomeration of the dispersed; 3) dispersion of the conglomerated; 4) dispersion of the dispersed; 5) whatever lingers between 1 and 4.}}

{{Are there communities of dust in virtual archives, for instance, after e-books have ousted the tomes that still line my shelves? Although countless other generators of dust persist, the virtualization of existence instills in us the illusion of a dust-free world. The spread of "virtual reality" throws plenty of dust into our eyes—in the first place, concerning the dwindling of dust. How much industrial pollution is hidden and displaced behind the translucent screens of virtual reality! How much dust must be spawned for one to believe that the dream of a dust-free life has finally come true!}}

{{*For a nonexistent dust jacket.* Dust to dust, and nothing shall come between the two! (Isn't "dust to dust" the only principle—if a principle it is—according to which a community of remnants shapes up?)}}

{{"Our constellation is buried in dust." Nelly Sachs[2]}}

{{The shapelessness of dust is the visual corollary to its openness: ever in position to add more to the clouds, balls, or layers in which it lies or flies and similarly prepared to part, to fall apart, letting go of its elements. But its openness is not that of a network, which relies on nodes, whence imaginary relations radiate or where they intersect.}}

{{*À la Foucault.* There are, according to *The Order of Things*, four notable types of similitude in sixteenth-century Europe: *convenientia, aemulatio,* analogy, and sympathy.[3] Each corresponds to a particular kind of grouping:

- *convenientia* draws things together based on their adjacency to one another in space;

- *aemulatio* is a mirror effect, whereby, for instance, the earth reflects the sky or what is above reflects what is below;

- analogy gauges the right proportion between the component parts;

- sympathies are dynamic attractions of things that share a common trait.

Can we extend this fourfold typology to the communities of dust?

1 *convenientia pulveris*: accidental nearness of animal dander, dust mites' feces, paper shreds, lint, etc., that have been left behind in the same place; mold spores, bacteria, pollen, dry soil, sand found in the vicinity of a fast-moving air-mass; mutual proximity of debris from a supernova explosion;

2 *aemulatio pulveris*: high and low: cosmic and household dust; the dust of the sky reflects that of the earth, and vice versa;

3 *analogia/ratio pulveris*: to the baser part of the human constitution corresponds the coarser of the elements (body dust earth);

4 *sympathia pulveris*: like draws like toward itself—the dust of the earth attracts the dust of our bodies (the scope of this attraction outstrips the planet's gravitational field); dust accumulates, layer upon layer, or swirls into balls, always remaining on the edge of separating.}}

{{The problem: Judeo-Christian expectations of resurrection here on earth are highly unsustainable. Given how overpopulated our planet is, we cannot fathom the nightmare of the roughly 80 billion human beings who have ever lived meeting all at once, in flesh and blood. The solution: resurrection (and togetherness) in dust.}}

{{If someone asks you for your membership card in communities of dust, you needn't show anything other than your physical existence. As philosophers like to say, that is the necessary and sufficient condition of possibility for joining such communities.}}

{{"I see myself isolated in the universe and wonder
   What effect I can have. My hands wave under
   The heavens like specks of dust that are floating asunder."
D. H. Lawrence[4]}}

{{Heidegger interpreted the Greek word *logos*—referring to discourse, speech, voice, articulation—as a "gathering gatheredness." Dust also gathers, albeit without actively gathering anything. Its community is a mere gatheredness. And it disperses just as easily, because it has no essence, tethering its parts to the whole through the bonds of necessity. Dust is the anti-*logos* (also within *logos* itself).}}

{{Will these lines coil into dust balls? If so, around what "infrastructures"? Will they pass like a cloud of a dust storm? Will they softly envelop your thought, adjusting to its contours? Will they retain their inconspicuousness on the floor, in the corners of a mental dwelling? Will they disperse into specks, for the most part invisible and inaudible?}}

{{"What matters it, my fairest and my best,
   That we go down unhonored and forgotten
   Into the dust, —so we descend together?
   Descend together, and then—and then perchance—"
Edgar Allan Poe[5]}}

{{A community of dusty remnants is non-hierarchical because it is beyond the purview of systematic classification. Differences between the byproducts of living beings, as much as between the animate and the inanimate, are expunged in it. Another revolutionary calculus is operative here:

   Freedom from identity +
   Equality in entropy and decay =
   Dusty fraternity.}}

{{Let's be crystal clear: Dust is not a symbol of anarchic communities. It is their all-too-real apotheosis.}}

{{Without unity (Corlett) and without co-immunity (Esposito), a community is *of dust*. This means that (a) it is made *out* of dust; (b) it belongs *to* dust; (c) it originates *in* dust; and (d) its mode of participation learns *from* and partakes of dust. Made of dust, a community has no determinate national, cultural, or even species character. Belonging to dust, it does not possess the world but is *a priori* appropriated to previously generated waste. Drawing its origins from dust, it has no clear origin but is, at best, traceable back to pulverized traces. Participating in and as dust, it depends on the fleeting, accidental, yet thoroughly material connections, in space and in time, that traverse the fields of dust.}}

{{"Now we feel nothing at all—only dust and ashes remain in us." Andrey Platonov[6]}}

{{*Forth and back.* The most rudimentary sense of community is togetherness. Together in a family, with friends or colleagues, in a state, or on earth, we are gathered. But we join—are joined to and by—the others through bonds that are precarious, fragile enough to get unfastened in an instant. Even in our closest relations (for example, when death intervenes between us). Becoming aware of this possibility, we stand a chance of finally encountering and being with each other, due to the gap that remains between us.

~

Back to dust! Different meanings, scales, and particles are gathered in it. But there is nothing in this togetherness that is guaranteed to last from one moment to the next; its meanings, scales, and particles can always discombobulate and disperse. I cannot imagine another way of being with others that would hinder so effectively the fusion of the one and the other in a "higher unity." Far from frivolous or insincere, togetherness in dust leaves the breathing space indispensable to constituting a *relation*.}}

{{*The memory of memory.* What remains of the work of mourning in a community of remnants? The object of mourning is the identity of a being irrevocably lost to us. Where something survives a past identity, from which this "something" has broken off, no mourning is due. Should we still associate dust with moribund realities, we ought to understand that the finitude it announces does not call for the work of mourning. At best, it might elicit the memory of mourning (or, if you will, the memory of memory).}}

{{A community of dust is the primal scene of and the postscript to being-in-touch.}}

{{To be included in a community, one must have something in common with others who (or that) participate in it. Communities of dust presuppose the lowest common denominator: materiality. They spring up from the terminable existence of material entities and the endurance of matter itself. Dust accumulates, precisely, in the difference between the infinite finitude of things and the finite infinity of matter.}}

{{*Uncanny accounting*. You do not lack what, unbeknownst to yourself, you consign to dust. Until, that is, your entire body becomes one with it. Another paradox: dust engenders a community of the most superfluous and the most indispensable.}}

{{The prefix *com-* in *community* is a modified version of the Latin word *cum*, "with." "With" is more basic still than "togetherness." In dust, wildly varied ingredients are with one another, but they are neither with the whole—that does not exist as such—nor with themselves. As much "with" as "without," a community of dust is a *semunity* (*sine*, or *se*, in composite words = without).}}

{{"True" infinity: circularity, completion:
  - Dust to dust.
 "Bad" infinity: a straight line, forever unfinished:
  - Dust to dust to dust to dust to dust to dust to . . .
 In the community of remnants "true" infinity is indistinguishable from "bad" infinity. The circle springs open into a straight line. The line bends into a circle. Opposites coincide. Non-dialectically.}}

{{*Solidarity & a common project*. Together in dust. To gather: in dust. To gather in: dust. To gathering dust. Gathering dust to . . .}}

{{Scarcely visible when taken in isolation, specks of dust that cling to one another, if provisionally, cannot be simply brushed off. The old adage of "strength in numbers" means, first of all, "visibility in numbers." In concert, dust specks obtrude onto our fields of vision; separately, they are out of sight. The same goes for human beings treated as though they were social and economic junk. In contrast to a lone panhandler on the street, it is no longer possible to make light of "the rabble," "the multitudes," a mass of "plebeians" ("the 99 percent"?). Their assemblages lack any and all organicity. In fact, they are born from the misery and destitution instigated by the destruction of all organic ties to the soil, to the place of birth, to the family, to a close-knit community. Togetherness from disintegration is, precisely, how dust accrues.}}

{{"The Dust behind I strove to join
  Unto the Disk before—
  But Sequence raveled out of Sound
  Like Balls upon a Floor—"
Emily Dickinson[7]}}

{{Community is a site of communication. What is communicated in the communities of remnants, within dust, or from dust to dust? What does an eyelash say, wordlessly, to minuscule bits of a sofa's *faux* leather, with which it mingles in the dust? Besides the possibility of a grouping unaccounted for by any system of classification, they convey (to one another, through their propinquity; and to us, assuming that we care to notice) finitude *and* survival, the afterlife of what appears to have disappeared, forever.}}

{{Aphoristic fragments are the dust specks of thought. They flock together as freely as they drift apart. If this entire book can be broken down into aphorisms, leaving its "meaning" unaffected, that is because the text before you is anything but a tightly woven textile; it is, conversely, a collection of unfastened threads, morsels, crumbs, *nano*-shards of experience. (Theodor Adorno's *Minima Moralia* is further titled "Reflections from a Damaged Life." A good second title for the book you are now reading would have been "Reflections from a Damaged Afterlife.") The ingredients of *Dust*, which you are now holding in your hands or scanning through on a computer screen, are the relics of the times and places where thinking happened and, in its very happening, disbanded into assertions, statements, theses, struggling to articulate, in vain, the elusive singularity of thinking. Thinking dust (as the subject and object of thought).}}

{{*Community's communion.* Biting (into) the dust.}}

{{In *Untimely Meditations*, Nietzsche complains that the surfeit of historical sense is a scourge of contemporary humanity. Too much memory and tradition stifle life. From the pre-Socratics onward, entire communities of intellectual dust have swelled and weighed on our consciousness (and the pre-Socratics, in turn, dubbed their predecessors *the ancients*!). When such communities are exceptionally crowded, we suffocate in their midst, breathing their dust right into the lungs of our thought. In the twenty-first century, Nietzsche's problem has been overturned; today, there is a dearth of historical sense. The age of mass media impresses on us that the 1990s have receded to ancient history. This predicament is hardly preferable to the malady of modernity. If the communities of intellectual dust are too sparse, they are no less suffocating than those that are overcrowded. Instead of being paralyzed by the awareness that "this has been done before," we act, blissfully ignorant of what we repeat, and commit worse errors than those of our predecessors.

—*P.S.* Referring to "intellectual dust" I am not reneging on the thesis that ideal objects, unlike material things, are *ideally* dust-free. What I have in mind is the materiality of thinking and of the communities of remnants it generates.}}

{{*Everything and nothing.* Dust is everything and nothing, having received particles from all that exists, but not having bestowed upon these particles a new determinate form. Dust is the medium, through which everything communes with the nothing it is about to become.}}

6 JUST DUST

We will enter the career
When our elders are no more!
There we shall find their dust [leur poussière]
And the trace of their virtues.
—FRENCH ANTHEM, *LA MARSEILLAISE*

the mere and the fair

Just dust. And nothing else besides this next-to-nothing. Just that has been absorbing our attention and even distraction in and between these lines. But there are also words—not the least among them, *dust* (or *dusting*, with which it all began) and *just*—that are, presumably, more than what they name. Do I hold onto them to stave off the relentless grinding away of time? In a belief that something other than just dust will remain?

When I say or write "just dust," I intend more than one thing simultaneously. First: mereness. Everything is just dust, regardless of the parade of forms beings assume.

Second (not as obviously as the first): fairness. Dust is just because it restores to beings their own, putting them in their rightful places within the vast expanse of matter. Stated this way, the two senses of *just*—the fact of bare existence and the norm of evenhandedness—overlap. Mereness is justice, to the extent that it keeps each thing within its limits, guarding against the distortions of idealization. Justice is mereness, insofar as it simply sorts things out according to the regions of being where they already belong in light of what they are. Injustice, for its part, is the extraneous addition of stratum upon stratum of meaning to the spatiotemporal existence of things. Contesting these superimpositions, phenomenological reduction (*epoché*) is the yearning for basic justice.

We should advance slowly and with caution from the juncture, at which we have just found ourselves. (". . . we have just found ourselves" reminds us of the third, temporal, sense of the word, according to which very little time has elapsed since an event. It occurred a split of a second ago and is still reverberating in our ears or lingering as an aftertaste on our tongues. At issue in *just dust*, then, is the evanescence of human life and, perhaps, of nonhuman existence as well. We have just emerged from dust and to it we are about to return.) The justice of mereness is in its affinity to equality. Although a mere lamp and a mere blade of grass are not one and the same thing, they are both shielded by their mereness from those metaphysical maneuvers that make them subservient to something they are not. A mere lamp and blade of grass do not have to conform to the fanciful molds into which we usually squeeze them. They are more equal to themselves without completely coinciding with themselves, without establishing an identity and self-identity—the worst of idealizations, the injustices metaphysics inflicts on mere things.[1]

At first blush, the assertion that the lamp and the grass and the dog and the human are just dust revives the notion that there is something beyond their mere heterogeneous existence. It appears that dust is their shared substance, a common and unstructured foundation that invalidates the differences among them, revealing their superficiality. Yet, depth is precisely what is missing from dust, bred on the surface of things and wedded to what they are in their finitude. Essentially superficial, dust cannot be abstracted from the things that fall into it. It is not the homogeneous residue of decay, but an intimate trace, a spatial testimony to the singular journey of each being through time.

Further misrepresentations of *just dust* may crop up. For one, mereness may deteriorate to banality and impute paltriness to the thing it predicates. There is a tinge of disappointment in our assessment of something as *just that*, which roughly means, "Nothing is happening here, or, at any rate, not much." *Just that* (for instance, just dust) does not count as an event or a being, even though one must have initially given it sufficient consideration to dismiss it out of hand. When we assess things this way we affirm their existence and, simultaneously, decline further engagement with them. It's just dust, and nothing more can be said on the subject. Case closed.

More often than not the reason for our dissatisfaction with mere things is that we crave the depth inaccessible to us in everyday life. The world contained within its own limits seems scant and faulty. Bereft of our fantasies and projections, it does not live up to our expectations. Mereness comes to signify privation—the relative lack of complexity, noteworthiness, or what have you. Hoping to unveil another world more appealing than our drab routine, we embark on a search for implicit nuances and secret signs that would point us in that other direction. Dust gauges this nonconformity of the real to our intentions, while its mereness surfaces as the symptom of our frustrations.

Some will hear in the expression *just dust* the resonances of nihilistic indifference. "If everything is 'just dust,' then why bother?" they will ask. But, lest we lapse into nihilism, we ought to inquire into the meaning of the copula *is* that articulates everything with dust. One of its senses is temporal. It is not that *now* only dust exists; the present tense of the verb *to be* surprisingly sends us back to the past and the future of dust. The second sense of the copula is constitutive. Dust is the residue that remains of everything that is and the elementary building block of sundry entities. My imaginary interlocutors will probably not object to these claims. What they will recoil from is the qualification *just* that—so the argument goes—razes temporal distinctions, formal differentiations and levels of complexity. In short, for them, the reality of just dust is impoverished and one-dimensional.

Ontological worries about mereness as banality are to a considerable extent complicit with ethico-political preoccupations with justice and equality as the indifference to . . . difference. Right-wing critics of equality in particular are apt to meld this term with the practice of equalization, a willful disregard of individual variations in ability, talent, merit, etc., that practically translates into a standard remuneration for all. Once relevant social policies are implemented, banality and mediocrity prevail, suffocating the spark of creativity and initiative in the ashes of society reduced to the lowest common denominator. Even Hélène Cixous, who is not allied to the political Right by any stretch of the imagination, lumps together equality, dust, and indifference in her description of Robben Island, where Nelson Mandela was imprisoned: "It was a day like the thirty thousand days before, so much the same, so gray of sky and sea, and for thirty thousand years nothing new under the sun of Robben Island. On the island all equally white with dust and all equal in non-hope."[2]

Incontestable is the conclusion that, in dust, differences between classes or categories of beings no longer matter. But to infer total indifference from the loss of the crudest markers of separation would be erroneous. Each component of dust adheres to its flitting community singularly, in accord with its distinctive temporal rhythm and constitution, its inimitable mode of emerging from and declining into matter. Only on the condition that we situate difference on the exclusive horizon of hierarchical organization will justice, equality, and, indeed, dust spell out a certain leveling-down, emblematic of nihilism. I daresay, however, that hierarchies are the main culprits in our indifference to subtle differences, which elude taxonomies and systems of classification. Mereness and fairness name, each in its own way, unclassifiable singularity, resistant to conceptual appropriation. In a word, just dust.

dust to dust

In referring to justice as a way to sort things according to their apposite regions of being, I've touched upon an ontological view, quite unfashionable and mainly forgotten nowadays. The crux of the argument delineated, above all, in Aristotle's *Physics*, is that bodies tend to return to their natural places, to the elements that are preponderant in their composition. A stone falls down to the earth, because the earthly element is its chief "material cause." The fire of the hearth rises up because celestial fire, which is its elemental home, is located above the earth, water, and even air. The movements of bodies according to nature ensure the harmony of the world, where everything is in its rightful place, or, if not, is on the way back to its ontological niche. Justice is the expression of cosmic concord, which includes what we now know as gravity, thermodynamics, and the other "laws" of physics. Or, better yet, it is the expression of love. (Aristotle's medieval commentator ibn Sīnā, whose Latinized name is Avicenna, took the striving and attraction of bodies to their natural places to be signs of an impersonal, universal love.)

Within this perfect system, dust has no region assigned to it.[3] Despite its association with the earth, dust can catch a ride on airflows and fly. It does not correspond squarely to the category of either life or death; neither does it pursue any goal nor fulfill any purpose in a teleological world-order. Its nature, within the parameters of the Aristotelian system, is *contra natura*. Outside the strictures of identity and under the guise of a tautology, it can only strive toward itself as wholly other to itself: dust to dust. Which is to say that it extends itself in numerous directions at any given time, because every region is, at bottom, "just" dust. Through it, the remains of every thing (singular) adhere to the remains of everything (universal). Dust operates an unfathomable shadow economy that may at times put a wrench in the wheels of teleological machinery.

When industrial production, powered by fossil fuels, works well according to its own standards, it increases the quantity of dust through its polluting side effects. *Homo faber* accelerates the journey of dust to dust and blows it up to planetary dimensions in the epoch of globalization. Unintended and undesirable, the generation of dust overshadows the manufacture of goods, which is the express goal of economic activity.[4] The tipping point of the environmental crisis occurs when the impact of dust's shadow economy turns out to be more far-reaching than that of the world's teleological workings. The planetary drifting of dust to dust overtakes the tending of the stone to the earth, or of the plant to solar heat and light.

A more charitable reading of the original Latin expression *pulverem pulveri*, rendered as *dust to dust* in the 1559 English *Book of Common Prayer*, beckons with the promise of redemption and resurrection. As the mourners in attendance throw handfuls of soil into the grave of the deceased, the text instructs the priest to announce:

> Forasmuche as it hath pleased almightie God of his great mercy to take upon hym selfe the Soule of oure deare brother, here departed, we therfore committe hys bodye to the grounde, earthe to earthe, ashes to ashes, dust to dust, in sure and certein hope of resurrection to eternall lyfe, throughe oure Lorde Jesus Christe, who shall chaunge oure vyle body that it may be lyke to hys glorious body, according to the mighty workynge, whereby he is able to subdue al thynges to hymselfe.[5]

How does committing "hys bodye to the grounde" pave the way to the "sure and certein hope of resurrection"? Although the three formulae that stand between death and resurrection—"earthe to earthe, ashes to ashes, dust to dust"—sound very much alike, they foretell contrasting futures to the body. On the one hand, "earthe to earthe" spurs the Aristotelian movement of restitution according to nature, such that an earthly human body returns to its native element. The same reunited with the same, the macro-order reconstitutes itself. "Dust to dust," on the other hand, interrupts the elemental cycle. Settling only for a little while, when everything is calm, it can be raised again at once as it swirls up into the air. Therefore, dust allegorizes the spiritualization of matter. Because of its restlessness and deconstruction of the boundaries between life and death, it reflects the hope of resurrection. (The growth of plants out of the ashes that fertilize the soil augurs a similar hopeful prospect.) Whereas an earthly thing's homecoming to the earth consolidates sameness, the dispensation of ashes to ashes and of dust to dust releases a nonidentity to a nonidentity, the other to the other, and death to "eternall lyfe." The alteration of the mortal and decaying body into a glorious one goes ahead *contra natura* thanks to the redemptive power of Christ, "the mighty workynge, whereby he is able to subdue al thynges to hymselfe." The "mighty workynge" of resurrection is pre-viewed, anticipated, if in a less spectacular fashion, in dust that cradles the vestiges of all things and releases light earth to the spirit-like domain of air.

Tempted as I am to accept the faint redemptive possibilities of dust and of fertilizing ashes, I am keenly aware that, in doing so, I would risk justifying the immolation of the earth on the pyres of religion, economy, or metaphysical philosophy. Different faiths are willing to concede a modicum of justice to death if, and only if, earthly mortality is dissociated from absolute finality.[6] So long as we do not reconcile ourselves with the mereness and fragility of the world, so long as we do not acquiesce to the (disappointing, to be sure) assertion that there is *just* this one and no other, we will keep sacrificing it to the pipe dreams of a higher reality, a more perfect existence, or life everlasting. The human onslaught on the earth, its ecosystems and life forms, is easily explicable in terms of creative destruction for the sake of transforming the merely given into the self-given, so that, in the end, Spirit would be able to recognize itself in the nature it has sublated, *aufgehoben*—hence my misgivings about the "redemptive" reading of dust. Where is the emancipatory potential of "fossil fuel burning, metal smelting, and waste incineration" that, in the twentieth century alone, "released thousands of tons of . . . toxic metals into the air as dust"[7]? Can we separate dust *from* dust, sift through its various kinds, and select those that are gentler, more poetic, or germane to redemption? Or, should we, instead, perceive in the ugliest, most harmful, and irredeemable dusty deposits (that have in the meantime permeated every cell in our bodies and in the organisms of all living beings) the main outlines of human history, rather than its regrettable repercussions? But then, again, perhaps only the irredeemable is worth the thought of redemption.

the revolutions of dust

On account of its semantic and physical instability, dust upends the relations of dominance and subordination, so much so that it becomes a symbol of revolution. This association is understandable, precisely because *revolution* is as volatile and unstable as dust itself.

Revolūtiō turns by rolling back; fundamentally conservative, it describes the rotation of a wheel or a celestial body in its orbit. The Platonic "moving image of eternity" and the Aristotelian reflux of things back to their "natural places" move in a similar trajectory. Only much later does revolution acquire the political sense we are familiar with and comes to denote the overthrow of a government. It was not until 1343 that an Italian chronicler, Giovanni Villani, imparted political significance to the word *revolution*, writing "*in così piccolo tempo la città ebbe tante novità e varie revoluzioni* [in such a short stretch of time, our city has experienced so much novelty and various revolutions]."[8] Like dust, revolutionary change involves multiple temporalities, from the regression to the past to the irruption of the radically new. Or, perhaps, it hints that what feels like *tante novità*, "so much novelty," is a thoroughly forgotten past event, recycled in another set of circumstances.

A curious double invocation of "the revolutions of dust" in a sermon by John Donne, dated 1620, weaves a net of political and cosmic proportions. "The knife, the marble, the skinne, the body are ground away, trod away, they are destroy'd, who knows the revolutions of dust?" Donne asks rhetorically. "Dust upon the Kings high-way, and dust upon the Kings grave, are both, or neither, Dust Royall, and may change places; who knows the revolutions of dust?"[9] Seeing that, irrespective of what they are, the fate of material entities—"the knife, the marble, the skinne, the body"—is to be ground away into dust, the hierarchy among them is redundant. Dust is the destiny and destination for everybody, whether organic or inorganic. Its revolutions are the rotations of the elements that used to be part of the marble, the skin, etc., within a framework of shared finitude.

Donne, nevertheless, rebuffs the idea that there is nothing but (actual or potential) dust. He wishes to preserve the hierarchical coupling of the body and the soul, the latter watching over the body during its earthly journey. "Even in the dead body of Christ Jesus himself," he writes, "one dram of the decree of his Father, one sheet, one sentence of the prediction of the Prophets preserv'd his body from corruption."[10] Were it not for the momentous difference between spirit and corporeity, a difference that originates outside finite existence *via* the intervention of metaphysical or theological constructs, the revolutions of dust would have swept everything in their path without delay—the knife, the marble, the skin, the king, and all. The divine Word is a stopgap against the "corrupting" flux of matter.

A human decree, in contrast, is powerless in the face of dust. In the sermon, Donne does not spare the king, who embodies the earthly political authority, from its metamorphoses. Absent any significant distinctions in matter, the high may be always brought low and the low elevated. The monarch, who is carried above the dust of the road today, may find himself under the dust of the cemetery tomorrow. "Dust upon the Kings high-way, and dust upon the Kings grave . . . may change places" in a rotation that superimposes the cosmic rhythm of matter's grinding away onto political history. This scheme does not lose any of its validity if the "natural" death of the monarch is substituted with social upheaval and revolutionary foment, which often culminated in regicide, as they did twenty-nine years after Donne's sermon, when Charles I was beheaded during the English Revolution. Whatever the form of government, the revolutions that destabilize it will be of dust. The slogan "The king is dead! Long live the king!" befits critical moments in monarchical succession, as much as the most diverse challenges to and re-normalizations of authority in general. For an ultra-brief interval between one monarch and another, between death and life, between the first exclamation mark and the second affirmation, or between competing political regimes, power itself is put in question and takes a dusting. Its perpetuity not assured, the very potentiality of power (the power of power) is shattered in the course of awaiting a fresh consolidation and a new rule.

Following the ineluctable dispersion of dust, its revolutions are a messy business, rife with tumult and chaos; they have little to do with the orderly rotation of the celestial spheres. We might say that they take place as the *elevation* or the *raising* of dust, an expression with three semantic slants: (1) a shift in political topology, whereby the low (those who live in and as dust, the "scum of the earth") become high and the high classes are lowered; (2) a resurrection of past hopes for change (as in "the raising of the body"); (3) the migration of dust from the earth to the air, whipping up a cloud from the residue that used to rest on a solid surface. So radical is the political earthquake (1) that it reconfigures the earth-air axis by sending plumes of dust upward (3) and reverses the flow of time by propelling frustrated aspirations into the future (2), putting the past ahead of us. Both in temporal and in spatial terms, the rhythm of the settling and the elevation, the resting and the flying, of dust enriches the fabric of metaphors that depict the relation between the status quo and the revolt.

Russian revolutionary Georgiy Plekhanov compares the proletarian uprising to unsettled dust. For him, "The scattered individual struggles of proletarians are . . . the molecular movement of a single, powerful social force. . . . The proletarians are 'human dust' flying into the eyes of the exploiters."[11] Plekhanov is right to think about the revolution as the disturbance of human dust. His formulation allows us to emphasize the dispersed unity of revolutionary struggles; the return of those who have been discarded as microscopic and hence insignificant garbage; the posthumous condition of the downtrodden; and the suffocating, blinding impact of the tumult on "the exploiters." It implies that revolutions are of dust in the double sense of the genitive: the objective and the subjective, transpiring in and galvanized by "human dust," which is another face or another surface of the Lukácsian subject-object of history (minus the totality).

Largely despite itself, Plekhanov's discourse also sheds light on the tragic outcome of revolutions. It reveals that they voice the demand for justice when it is already too late for the victims of economic, political, cultural, and temporal shredding machines that reduce us to dust. It permits the exploiters, whose eyes are irritated in the tumult, to keep their human countenance. And it conveys that, after a period of unrest, dust will surely settle, things will get back to normal, often with only a few cosmetic changes. This should not come as news to anyone acquainted either with the history of radical political movements or with the etymology of "revolution" that underscores cyclical fluctuations. Plekhanov's fervor ought to be tempered with Donne's more pensive question: "Who knows the revolutions of dust?"

7 DUSTART

She missed the roses. They had left an empty space inside her. Remove an object from a clean table and by the cleaner patch that remains you see that there was dust all around it. The roses had left a patch without dust and without sleep inside her.
—CLARICE LISPECTOR, *FAMILY TIES*

ready-unmade

With unmatched elegance, in a few lines of the short story "The Imitation of the Rose," Lispector sketches out an allegory of modern art. As a rule, a work of art classified as modern highlights the (material) conditions of possibility for perception and, in so doing, elucidates *aesthēsis* as such. Impressionism is probably the most salient movement in this regard, interested more in *how* landscapes, objects, and people appear than in *what* is to be represented of the real. Minimalism, in music and in painting, is a worthy inheritor of the artists' fascination with the very stuff of which both perception and art are made. Mark Rothko's works—for instance, *Red on Maroon* (1959)—depict color and its hues or shades. They radicalize the thrust of, say, Henri Matisse's *The Red Studio* (1911), which was still crowded with identifiable objects, even if the main "hero" of the painting was the color red. Musical compositions by Philip Glass, Steve Reich, Henrick Górecki, or Arvo Pärt put sound itself at the forefront. And so forth.

Modern art relegates the forms of things to the background (and, at times, to the space outside the frame), while foregrounding the materials of which artworks are made. This emptying out is featured in the episode with the roses Lispector narrates in her story.[1] The disappearance of the flowers adored by the main character corresponds to the evaporation of all objective outlines and leaves a gaping hole at the heart of the subject. A modern artwork removes objects from the "clean table" of mimesis and representation, revealing thereby the persistence of matter, which is dust. It does not put materiality under the microscope or in the spotlight; what it illuminates, instead, is the void—the absence of form, emptiness, an uncanny clearing—in contrast to which the previously imperceptible matter/dust comes into view.

The gamble of modernist aesthetics is that the materiality of art would announce itself in the disappearance of objective form. But when the pendulum swings back to the subject, absence spins out of control, blinding us yet another time to the dusty remnants of matter. We have heard Lispector say that the "roses had left a patch without dust and without sleep inside her." Accompanied by insomniac vigilance, the obliteration of dust within her is in tandem with the receding external dust. The absence of form becomes a fixation, an "absence that flooded into her like a light. And also around the mark left by the roses the dust was disappearing. The center of fatigue opened itself into a circle that grew larger."[2] The shock of the object's withdrawal wears off in the measure that we get accustomed to its non-presence. What the missing piece had obliquely brought to our attention has been now swallowed into inconspicuousness. Absence turns into a shining fetish, presented and re-presented *ad nauseam* in modern art and thought.

How can we hold onto the vanishing so that it would neither itself vanish nor undergo a cycle of idealization (or idolization)? How can we avow its alliance with matter? By consigning it to dust, or by assigning dust to it. That is what Marcel Duchamp and Man Ray did in *Dust Breeding*, or *Élevage de Poussière* (1920). For a year, Duchamp let dust accumulate on the back of his massive 2.75 meter-tall work *The Bride Stripped Bare by Her Bachelors, Even* (1915–23), alternatively titled *The Large Glass*. When the layer of dust was thick enough, Ray visited Duchamp's Broadway studio in New York that housed the piece placed by an open window. There, he photographed the resulting "ready-made" with a two-hour exposure, so as to capture the fine grains of city pollution mixed with the puffs of cotton and other vestiges of the artist's year of life and work.

FIGURE 1 Marcel Duchamp and Man Ray, *Dust Breeding* (1920). Image copyright © The Metropolitan Museum of Art. Image source: Art Resource. © Man Ray Trust/Artists Rights Society (ARS), NY/ADAGP, Paris 2015.

The intricate play of concealing and revealing, of denuding and veiling, in part facilitated by dust, was deliberate. Ray recalls: "While the bride lay on her face decked out in her bridal finery of dust and debris, I exposed her to my sixteen-candle camera."[3] The sexual innuendo of the explanation is blatant. *The Bride* . . . was covered in dust, only to be exposed once again before the photographic lens, and following a "long exposure" procedure at that. The disappearance of "her" form leaves behind a void, which becomes the subject of *Dust Breeding* and motivates a slew of interpretations, some of them fueled by the artists' claim that the depicted image was of a "view taken from an airplane by Man Ray." As identifiable outlines and orientational markers wane, dust breeds new hermeneutical possibilities immersed in the materiality of the work. Duchamp and Ray blanket the absence of things, as well as of a fixed referent to be represented, with the "bridal finery" of debris, instead of concentrating, as Lispector does, on the dust that surrounds a missing object. Their aesthetic matrix is, nonetheless, analogous: the evacuation of form gives way to the materialization of dust.

Breeding is a sexual process, anticipated in the encounter of the bride and her bachelors. The word *élevage*, "raising," in the original French title is far from elevated; it evokes primarily farming practices, as in *élevage de bovins*, or cattle breeding. According to his statement, Duchamp intended *Élevage de Poussière* in much the same sense as "Raising Pigs,"[4] which speaks to his effort to bring art from the ethereal peaks of Parnassus down to earth. Dust breeding, in turn, multiplies life's remains, morsels of survival, traces of death in life and life in death. It does so in an erotic fashion, through an intercourse between the existing artwork, the minuscule remnants it supports, and the aesthetic production of an opaque, dusty screen for fantasy and imagination.

In and behind the scene we are witnessing, the piece *The Bride* . . . is the bride. Duchamp and Ray are the bachelors; they resort to the obverse of a formed *chef-d'oeuvre* to provide a material footing for their photographic gaze. Between the bride and the bachelors, the dust of New York City and the studio intervenes. Intentionally or unintentionally, but at any rate mutely, the bachelors and the bride collect, document, and account for the scraps of life, world, and work. In seizing this record, the duo Duchamp-Ray reanimates it. They resurrect the potentiality for resurrection buried in the dust. *Élevage* is inextricably tied to *élevation*. Dust raising is dust rising.

Ray hints at the broader significance of the photographs, writing that, in them, "was fixed, once and for all, the *Domaine de Duchamp*."[5] Rather than a domain of ready-mades, such as the famous 1917 *Fountain*, it is one of ready-unmades, of things frayed to dust. The artists couple their creativity with the fecundity and generativity of entropy so as to, subsequently, give birth to the dusty materiality of art. Because the unmaking of the world is already under way, their own practice merely evinces its outcomes. Hence, the sexual undercurrents of *Dust Breeding* coexist with a certain celibacy and noninterference—the back-and-forth of denuding and covering up; references to the yet unconsummated relation between the bride and the bachelors; an indeterminate slippage in titles from *The Bride* . . . to a more neutral *The Large Glass*.

The photographs taken, Duchamp swabbed down *The Large Glass* and did away with much of the dust that had gathered on its superficies, albeit not all of it. Were he to destroy the archive, he would have surrendered, outside the frame, to the cleaners' tendency to delete the inscription of finitude, along with the place where it is etched. Instead,

Duchamp preserved dust in a section of the work by combining it with varnish to create "an effect of blond, transparent cones which I never would have obtained with paint."[6] The ready unmade was permanently integrated into *The Bride . . .*, already generated and, virginally, on the verge of breeding.

stardust twilight

Walter Benjamin's iconic essay on "The Work of Art in the Age of Mechanical Reproducibility" (1936) sounds the death knell of auratic art. The aura was an attribute of traditional artworks that, while admitting the possibility of replication, were singular because entirely embedded in their contexts. More often than not, they were uniquely situated in a cathedral or a theater, and the human approach to them was inflected with sacred reverence, linked to the cult function they served. In modern art Benjamin diagnoses the "decay of the aura."[7] A film, a photograph, or a sound recording are produced as reproducible and disembedded from the contexts where we might view them or listen to them. Consequently, neither the perceived object nor the perceiver fit the traditional model: "To pry an object from its shell, to destroy its aura, is the mark of a perception whose 'sense of the universal equality of things' has increased to such a degree that it extracts it even from a unique object by means of reproduction."[8] The metaphor of a hidden kernel within the object's shell is no longer appropriate to a reproducible work of art that thrives on exposure and distraction, not on the difficulty of access and patient concentration. In the era of mechanical reproducibility, art and its reception must be essentially superficial, which is to say that they must be dust-like. Hence, the "sense of the universal equality of things" Benjamin mentions in his analysis.

At the dawn of sound movies, Benjamin could not have known how aura would mutate, rather than decay, in late modernity. From the fact that, in a studio, "the camera is substituted for the public," he deduced that "the aura that envelops the actor vanishes, and with it the aura of the figure he portrays."[9] But, if anything, the auratic effect is amplified when the actors themselves are not present, or, better, when they are present only as projections on screen and as the screens for our fantasies. It is true that in those cases there is no such thing as an aura, and yet its privation does not impede the spread of stardust, into which the enchanting emanations of tradition have crumbled.

The word *stardust* displays a staggering range of meanings, from the faraway stars, too distant to be seen individually, to a magical or charismatic quality or feeling ("especially in the context of success in the world of entertainment or sports," one of the *Oxford Dictionaries* specifies[10]); from a slang designation for drugs (particularly, cocaine and phencyclidine) to a romantic, dreamlike state ("to have stardust in one's eyes"); from dust formed as a result of supernova explosions to a magical shiny powder. Many of these significations converge on celebrity in the epoch of reproducibility that is not only mechanical but also digital. But, first, we need to look into the main differences between "aura" and "stardust."

Following Benjamin's rendition of the term, aura resembles a stable aureole, encircling the artwork and integrating it into a powerful, magnet-like unity with its environmental context. Auratic art is a bottomless vortex of singularity that draws the spectator into itself. Stardust, on the contrary, disperses from the celebrity outward. It does not involve the spectator in itself, but rubs off thanks to our proximity to the star, either accidental or sought after. Frequently, it is disseminated fetishistically, through the personal effects of famous personalities auctioned off at extravagant prices and valuable, precisely, as exceptions to the regime of reproducibility that confirm the general rule. If both the aura and stardust have a magical feel to them, the latter is not due to the work of art as such but to the conflation between a pure representation devoid of original presence and the actual bodies of actors, singers, or sportswomen/sportsmen who can never live up to the ideal they are associated with. Stardust emanates from the unresolved tension between these extremes, consuming the physical or mental existence of the star ground to dust. In this, too, it is distinct from the aura, an emanation that miraculously does not deplete (and, in fact, safeguards) the original.

The spread of stardust foretokens death, as movie director Sandy Bates, the protagonist of Woody Allen's *Stardust Memories* (1980) posthumously understands after being shot by a fan at a retrospective of his films. Although Bates only thinks that he is dead, later to regain consciousness in the emergency room, his posthumous perspective extends beyond the aftermath of the attack and is generally synonymous with fame. The filmmaker's material existence, which he deems meaningless, is jarringly at odds with his celebrity. The clash between the two—the absurdity of the real and the hyperinflation of the ideal; a flesh-and-blood human being and a face, body, or voice reproducible on a video or audio recording—whips up clouds of stardust. Bates is granulated into it, mobbed by fans eager to get a hold of his time and objects "for charity." The implication is that, symbolically, the adoring crowds are the accomplices in his murder. The fan who shoots him at close range (shouting, "Sandy, you know you are my hero!") merely finishes the job and brutally resolves the opposition between the real and the ideal.

Allen makes explicit the connection between stardust and physical dust in a monologue that aligns the disintegration of the world with the much more trivial fading of art and fame. The retrospective, with its open criticism of Bates's later films, forces him to reexamine his artistic production, as well as the universe itself, *sub specie pulveris*: "Hey, did anybody read on the front page of *The Times* that matter is decaying? Am I the only one that saw that? The universe is gradually breaking down. There's not gonna be anything left. I'm not talking about my stupid little films here. Eventually, there's not gonna be any Beethoven or Shakespeare or . . ."

FIGURE 2 Film poster for *Stardust Memories* (1980), directed by Woody Allen. © Courtesy Everett Collection/Rex.

If dust remembers seemingly indestructible matter, then stardust recollects the ostensibly everlasting aura. But that is not all: *Stardust Memories* takes an extra step of delivering even stardust and dust to memory, and so inches toward absolute forgetting and destruction. "There's not gonna be anything left"—not even dust nor the memory of memory— is an apt summary of the materialist tragedy not so different from the idealist conviction that everything will be preserved, elsewhere. A timeless remembrance and an abiding forgetting are equally dust- and stardust-free. They infinitely pass into one another beyond the confines of consciousness.

The expectation of an imminent end of the world also sets the stage for David Bowie's persona Ziggy Stardust. Launched in 1972, the album *The Rise and Fall of Ziggy Stardust and the Spiders from Mars* propelled Bowie to international fame. For his celebrity to live on, however, Ziggy Stardust had to die, as the singer explained to William Burroughs in an extensive interview published in the February 28, 1974, issue of *Rolling Stone* magazine. For Bowie (or for Ziggy), it all begins with the news of an impending global apocalypse: "The time is five years to go before the end of the earth. It has been announced that the world will end because of lack of natural resources." But, in Ziggy's case, the

end comes when the infinites arrive. They really are a black hole, but I've made them people because it would be very hard to explain a black hole on stage. . . . When the infinites arrive, they take bits of Ziggy to make themselves real, because in their original state they are anti-matter and cannot exist in our world. And they tear him to pieces on stage during the song "Rock 'n' Roll Suicide." As soon as Ziggy dies on stage the infinites take his elements and make themselves visible.[11]

The reference to stardust, incorporated into Ziggy's very name, alludes both to cosmic phenomena and to his fame.

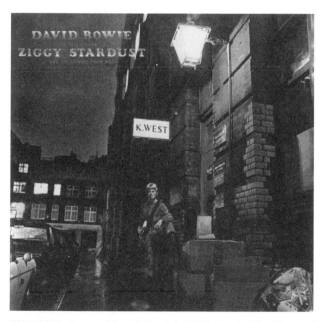

FIGURE 3 Cover of David Bowie's 1972 album, *The Rise and Fall of Ziggy Stardust and the Spiders from Mars*.

When he is shredded to pieces, each of them giving body to the singularities of black holes, the two senses merge into one. Prior to his physical dispersion and transubstantiation, the name already indicates the scattering of his identity, rendering indeterminate the lines that demarcate authenticity from inauthenticity (Bowie and his persona), or masculinity from femininity (Ziggy is an androgynous character). The strangely appealing "incoherence of his public face," compared to the "traditional rock idols of the 1960s,"[12] is a spin-off of stardust, taken up into and sprinkled from the name itself. We are smack in the middle of stardust twilight—the zone of indistinction, uncertainty, oscillation, wavering.

With regard to Allen's Sandy Bates and Bowie's Ziggy Stardust, the unanswered question is why the movie director and the rock star need to produce works of art, whose central heroes are a movie director and a rock star, respectively. A simplistic response is that the fictional or semi-fictional characters function as the autobiographic avatars of their creators and, thus, reveal their actual brushes with stardom and the fallout from fame that grinds them into stardust. Such an explanation is deficient to the extent that it disregards the fantastic, grotesque, and unconscious elements of each artwork. More attractive, to my taste, is the conclusion that Allen's and Bowie's "stardust personae" are either their defense mechanisms, or the apparatuses of wish fulfillment, or both simultaneously.

Assuming, on the one hand, that Sandy Bates and Ziggy Stardust are their ingenuous protective masks, both artists elide the destructiveness of fame that is inevitable in any direct confrontation between a reproducible ideal and the living-breathing human being associated with it. Instead of saying to the public, *hoc est corpus meum*, "Here is my body," they offer the body of a stand-in, an aesthetic double, closer to the corpus of their work than to their so-called private lives. An elaborate hocus-pocus, a substituting trick, allows them to sacrifice these dummies to the star-grinders and star-shredders of the day. If, on the other hand, Sandy and Ziggy are there to enact Allen's and Bowie's wish fulfillment, then they are the magnifying lenses for fame, which attains an almost superhuman pitch in them, and, at the same time, fantasies of suicide by one's own celebrity. Since this death wish is satisfied in the aesthetic sphere, it, too, participates in a network of defense mechanisms, charged with shielding the ego and the body from a direct imposition of the ideal. Even in imagining the ultimate putrefaction of reality, the art and the thinking of dust (including, of course, stardust) defer the instant when everything would dissolve into fine-grained, chalky waste.

making space in dust

Whereas, nearly a century ago, Duchamp permanently affixed dust to a relatively small portion of *The Large Glass*, contemporary DustArt has inverted the part-whole relation. Today, works of art appear in the interstices of dusty surfaces, through strokes that subtract minute quantities of dust, rather than add it to the canvas. Sense germinates when the artist makes a little space in (choreo-graphs) the gray infrastructure of the world, temporarily clearing some of the dust from the work. Obviously, the reason for this inversion is that in order to live—and not just to produce art—we must struggle to open pockets of existence in the overwhelmingly polluted milieus of earth, water, and air. A previously unheard-of phenomenology is shaping up here. Dust no longer draws our attention to the space it inconspicuously fills; instead, the rare interstitial spaces in it give us the glimmers (or the afterglows) of meaning. Dust has become the medium and the message, the background and the figure. The world looks more and more like a dusty windshield, except that there is no transparent support underneath layers of dirt. It is dust all the way down. Given the combination of matter liberated from the constraints of spirit and pollution making the environment less and less propitious to life, all we can hope to achieve is to scratch the surface of the surface and, plowing through dust, disclose a smidgeon of meaning. Heidegger's unconcealment (*alētheia*) is not a clearing in the woods but a furrow of sense in the fields of dry rot.

American artist Allison Cortson exemplifies this trend. In a series of portraits titled *Dust Paintings*, she uses predominantly the dust collected from the vacuum cleaners of her subjects' homes, which she "sprinkle[s] on the canvas and manipulate[s] with a brush."[13] The paintings are literally crafted out of dust, which is then set in place with an acrylic

FIGURE 4 Allison Cortson, *Eric and His Dust* (2009). Reproduced with permission of the artist.

sealer, the only exception being the human figure itself, rendered with oil paints. It could well be that the exemption Cortson grants to her subjects is a sign of her metaphysical nostalgia for the time when dust did not claim everything. The important point, though, is not so much the quantitative presence of household waste in her works as the tight grip, in which it holds the representing, the represented, and the medium of representation.

In *Eric and His Dust* (2009) denim-clad Eric, his blue clothes contrasting with the gray interiors, turns away from the spectators to quietly contemplate balls of dust gathered on the floor of his dwelling. Depicted on canvas, dust is something we, along with Eric, stare at. But what performs the depicting, what puts aesthetic representation to work, is the actual dust from his house. Moreover, since this singular material (or matter, which is, by the grace of art, also form) derives from Eric's body and the contents of his abode, we see, essentially, dust staring at itself. His dust is more than itself—at once, a self-representation and the reconstituted fabric of the place where it initially accumulated.

Alexandre Orion, a Brazilian artist known for urban interventions, often avails himself of city pollution to create series such as *Polugrafia* (2009) or *Poluição sobre muro* (*Pollution on the Wall*, 2012). In *Ossário* (2006), Orion deployed the technique of reverse graffiti to cover a 300-meter extension of a traffic tunnel in the city of São Paulo with countless skulls. More precisely, he *uncovered* the silhouettes by removing patches of soot and dust from tunnel walls. Pollution, then, provided the backdrop for the images and contributed to the play of light and shadow in them. Orion's reverse graffiti made sense of a wall of dust by subtracting smidgeons of accumulated matter from its surface. Converted into an ossuary (*ossário*) with human skulls piled one of top of the other, the dark space of the tunnel lit up with meaning. It intimated that one of the consequences of city life is a mass reproduction of death, our lungs (much like the underground passage) invaded with grime and dust.

FIGURE 5 Alexandre Orion, *Ossário* (2006). Reproduced with the permission of the artist.

To a certain extent and to the chagrin of Kantian purists, DustArt encourages a utilitarian form of aesthetics, instigated by environmental concerns. Cortson's paintings, for example, recycle household dust, while Orion's interventions force the Brazilian authorities to reluctantly take care of polluted urban spaces (his tunnel works are invariably hosed down from municipal trucks in what amounts to censorship with an environmental upside). Yet, their immediate ecological impact dims in comparison to the provocations they address to our senses and to sense, that is to say, to *aesthēsis*. DustArt approximates the real as it scribbles on a substratum comprised of the dusty traces of things. It corroborates our suspicion that reality is not a hard and unchipped rock, against which we throw meaning and ourselves in vain, but loose residue on a surface without depth. Futile are attempts to pin labels onto its fickle components. The strategy of DustArt is much more effective than that: to wade through the particles of the real and to impress our fragile, inherently erasable marks on its outermost coating. To make space in dust, while ridding ourselves of the expectation that the interstices would stay open indefinitely. To stop running away from the dustbin of history. To breathe there, finally.

NOTES

Chapter 1

1 Carolyn Steedman [*Dust: The Archive and Cultural History* (New Brunswick, NJ: Rutgers University Press, 2002), 160–1] has already commented on the "bifurcated meaning" of the word dust. Her explanation of its "strange semantic circularities," however, hinges on the Freudian notion of the uncanny.

2 Henry David Thoreau, *Walden, or Life in the Woods* (Mineola, NY: Dover Publications, 1995), 23.

3 Friedrich Nietzsche, "Thus Spoke Zarathustra," in *The Portable Nietzsche*, edited by Walter Kaufmann (New York and London: Penguin, 1954), 129.

4 Gunilla Norris, *Being Home: Discovering the Spiritual in the Everyday* (Mahwah, NJ: HiddenSpring, 2002), 25.

5 Julia Alvarez, *Homecoming* (New York: Penguin, 1984), 9.

6 Sigmund Freud, "Beyond the Pleasure Principle," in *The Standard Edition of the Complete Psychological Works of Sigmund Freud*, Volume 18, translated and edited by James Starchey (London: Vintage, 2001), 36ff.

7 Annie Dillard, *For the Time Being* (New York: Vintage, 1999), 123.

Chapter 2

1 Charles Rockwell Lanman, *A Sanskrit Reader: Text and Vocabulary with Notes* (Cambridge, MA: Harvard University Press, 1884), 178.

2 N. V. Voroshchinnikov, "In the Kitchen of Dust Modeling," in *Optics of Cosmic Dust*, edited by Gorden Videen and Miroslav Kocifaj (Dordrecht: Kluwer, 2002), 1–2.

3 Karen Barad, *Meeting the Universe Halfway: Quantum Physics and the Entanglement of Matter and Meaning* (Durham, NC and London: Duke University Press, 2007), 107.

4 Nanna Bjørnholt Karlsson, "Mars Has Belts of Glaciers Consisting of Frozen Water," University of Copenhagen news release, April 7, 2015, http://news.ku.dk/all_news/2015/04/mars-has-belts-of-glaciers-consisting-of-frozen-water/.

5 Ghassan Zaqtan, *Like a Straw Bird It Follows Me, and Other Poems*, translated by Fady Joudah (New Haven, CT: Yale University Press, 2012), 98.

6 Jean-Paul Sartre, "Intentionality: A Fundamental Idea of Husserl's Phenomenology," in *The Phenomenology Reader*, edited by Dermot Moran and Timothy Mooney (London and New York: Routledge, 2002), 383. I thank Edward S. Casey for helpfully pointing out this reference.

7 Sartre, "Intentionality," 382.

8 Sartre, "Intentionality," 383.

9 Kay Römer, "Tracking Real-World Phenomena with Smart Dust," in *Wireless Sensor Networks: First European Workshop, EWSN 2004*, Volume 1, edited by Holger Karl, Andreas Willig, and Adam Wolisz (Berlin and Heidelberg: Springer, 2004), 28.

10 William James, *The Principles of Psychology*, Volume 1 (Mineola, NY: Dover, 1950), 149–50.

11 James, *The Principles of Psychology*, 161.

12 Marcel Proust, *Remembrance of Things Past*, Volume II, translated by C. K. Scott Moncrieff and Stephen Hudson (London: Wordsworth, 2006), 1210.

13 Martin Heidegger, *Being and Time* (San Francisco: HarperCollins, 1964), 83.

14 Andrew Delahunty and Sheila Dingen, eds, "Samarra," in *Oxford Dictionary of Reference and Allusion* (Oxford: Oxford University Press, 2012), 317.

Chapter 3

1 John Donne, *The Sermons of John Donne*, edited by Evelyn M. Simpson and George Potter, Volume X (Oakland, CA: University of California Press, 1962), 187.

2 Wallace Stevens, *Selected Poems*, edited by John N. Serio (New York: A. A. Knopf, 2009), 271.

3 Cf. the epigraph to the current chapter.

4 Joseph Brodsky, *Collected Poems in English* (New York: Farrar, Straus and Giroux, 2002), 49.

5 Clarice Lispector, *Um Sopro de Vida* (Rio de Janeiro: Editora Nova Fronteira, 1978), 34.

6 Nola Taylor Redd, "Violent Star Explosion Reveals Origins of Space Dust," July 10, 2014, http://www.space.com/26482-cosmic-dust-survives-star-explosions.html, last accessed on December 22, 2014.

7   Christa Gall, Jens Hjorth, et al., "Rapid Formation of Large Dust Grains in the Luminous Supernova 2010jl," *Nature* 511 (July 2014): 326–29.

8   Friedrich Nietzsche, *Gay Science*, edited by Bernard Williams (Cambridge: Cambridge University Press, 2001), 194.

9   Mahmoud Darwish, *If I Were Another: Poems*, translated by Fady Joudah (New York: Farrar, Straus and Giroux, 2009), 137.

10   Darwish, *If I Were Another*, 47.

11   Mahmoud Darwish, *In the Presence of Absence*, translated by Sinan Antoon (New York: Archipelago, 2011), 115.

Chapter 4

1   Cf. Jacques Derrida, *Rogues: Two Essays on Reason*, translated by Michael Naas and Pascale-Anne Brault (Stanford: Stanford University Press, 2005), *passim*.

2   Jacques Derrida, *Writing and Difference*, translated by Alan Bass (Chicago and London: University of Chicago Press, 1980), 127ff. For instance, "the other as *res* is simultaneously less other (not absolutely other) and less 'the same' than I."

3   Emmanuel Levinas, "The Trace of the Other," in *Deconstruction in Context: Literature and Philosophy*, edited by Mark C. Taylor (Chicago and London: University of Chicago Press, 1986), 346.

4   Luce Irigaray and Michael Marder, *Through Vegetal Being* (New York: Columbia University Press, 2016).

5   John F. Mongillo and Linda Zierdt Washaw, *Encyclopedia of Environmental Science* (Santa Barbara, CA: Greenwood, 2000), 137.

6 Mary Douglas, *Purity and Danger: An Analysis of Concepts of Pollution and Taboo* (New York and London: Routledge, 2002), 44ff.

7 Joseph A. Amato, *Dust: A History of the Small & the Invisible* (Berkeley and Los Angeles: University of California Press, 2000), 81.

8 Ann G. Miguel, Glen R. Cass, et al., "Allergens in Paved Road Dust and Airborne Particles," *Environmental Science & Technology*, 33(23) (1999): 4159–68.

9 Julie Cart, "Officials Study Valley Fever Outbreak at Solar Power Projects," *Los Angeles Times*, April 30, 2013, http://articles.latimes.com/2013/apr/30/local/la-me-solar-fever-20130501.

10 Martin Heidegger, *Poetry, Language, Thought*, translated by Albert Hofstadter (New York: HarperCollins, 2001), 144ff.

Chapter 5

1 Percy Bysshe Shelley, *The Poetical Works*, Volume II, edited by H. Buxton Forman (London: Reeves & Turner, 1892), 29.

2 Nelly Sachs, "Chorus of the Rescued," in *Truth and Lamentation: Stories and Poems on the Holocaust*, edited by Milton Teichman and Sharon Leder (Champaign, IL: University of Illinois Press, 1994), 279.

3 Michel Foucault, *The Order of Things: An Archaeology of the Human Sciences* (London and New York: Routledge, 1989), 20–7.

4 David Herbert Lawrence, *Complete Poems* (London and New York: Penguin, 1993), 223.

5 Edgar Allan Poe, *The Complete Works of Edgar Allan Poe in Ten Volumes*, Volume 6 (Akron, OH: The Werner Company, 1908), 93–4.

6 Andrey Platonov, *The Foundation Pit*, translated by Robert Chandler and Olga Meerson (New York: NYRB Classics, 2009), 104.

7 Helen Vendler, *Dickinson: Selected Poems and Commentaries* (Cambridge, MA: Harvard University Press, 2010), 359.

Chapter 6

1 For more on the philosophical import of mereness, consult Simon Critchley, *Things Merely Are: Philosophy in the Poetry of Wallace Stevens* (London and New York: Routledge, 2005).

2 Hélène Cixous, *The Hélène Cixous Reader*, edited by Susan Sellers (London and New York: Routledge, 1994), 179.

3 Refer to the out-of-placeness of dust, which we monitored in Chapter 4.

4 Actually, in the capitalist regime of production, material products are not the ends; they are but the means for the self-augmentation of value. It is not by chance that the desired and the obnoxious ramifications of capitalist industry—money and dust—go hand in hand.

5 *The Book of Common Prayer: The Texts of 1549, 1559, and 1662,* edited by Brian Cummings (Oxford: Oxford University Press, 2011), 172.

6 Citing Hosea 13:14, Paul's exclamation in 1 Corinthians 15:55 "Where, O death, is your victory? Where, O death, is your sting?" is the paramount example here, but the belief in reincarnation is also pertinent.

7 J. R. McNeill, *Something New under the Sun: An Environmental History of the Twentieth-Century World* (London and New York: W. W. Norton, 2001), 54.

8 Giovanni Villani, *Cronica di Giovanni Villani: A miglior lezione ridotta coll'aiuto de' testi a penna*, Volume 7 (Florence: Il Magheri, 1823), 61. I thank Artemy Magun for this reference.

9 John Donne, *The Sermons of John Donne*, edited by Evelyn M. Simpson and George Potter, Volume III (Oakland, CA: University of California Press, 1957), 105–6.

10 Donne, *The Sermons of John Donne*, 106.

11 Quoted in Vladimir Petrovich Akimov, *Vladimir Akimov on the Dilemmas of Russian Marxism, 1895–1903*, edited by Jonathan Frankel (Cambridge: Cambridge University Press, 1969), 114.

Chapter 7

1 See the epigraph to this chapter, drawn from Clarice Lispector, *Family Ties*, translated by Giovanni Pontiero (Austin, TX: University of Texas Press, 2003), 68.

2 Lispector, *Family Ties*, 69.

3 Neil Baldwin, *Man Ray: American Artist* (New York: De Capo Press, 2000), 71.

4 Baldwin, *Man Ray*, 72.

5 Baldwin, *Man Ray*, 72.

6 Baldwin, *Man Ray*, 72.

7 Walter Benjamin, *Illuminations: Essays and Reflections* (New York: Schocken Books, 1968), 222.

8 Benjamin, *Illuminations*, 223.

9   Benjamin, *Illuminations*, 229.

10 Cf. "Stardust," in *Oxford American Large Print Dictionary*, edited by Erin McKean (Oxford and New York: Oxford University Press, 2006), 1188.

11 Craig Copetas, "Beat Godfather Meets Glitter Mainman: William Burroughs, Say Hello to David Bowie," *Rolling Stone* 155 (February 28, 1974): 24–7.

12 Chris Rojek, *Celebrity* (London: Reaktion Books, 2004), 135.

13 Allison Cortson, "Dust Paintings," http://www.allisoncortson.com/dust-paintings.html.

INDEX

Page references for illustrations appear in *italics*.